DISTRIBUTION OF INCOME: EAST AND WEST

PROFESSOR DR. F. DE VRIES LECTURES

DISTRIBUTION OF INCOME: EAST AND WEST

PETER WILES

Professor of Economics
University of London

1974

NORTH-HOLLAND PUBLISHING COMPANY – AMSTERDAM • OXFORD
AMERICAN ELSEVIER PUBLISHING COMPANY, INC. – NEW YORK

Library of Congress Catalog Card Number 74–76883
ISBN North-Holland for this series 0 7204 3400 9
ISBN North-Holland for this volume 0 7204 3409 2
ISBN American Elsevier 0 444 10683 9

Publishers:

NORTH-HOLLAND PUBLISHING COMPANY - AMSTERDAM
NORTH-HOLLAND PUBLISHING COMPANY, LTD. - OXFORD

Sole distributors for the U.S.A. and Canada:

AMERICAN ELSEVIER PUBLISHING COMPANY, INC.
52 VANDERBILT AVENUE
NEW YORK, N.Y. 10017

PRINTED IN THE NETHERLANDS

Professor F. de Vries (1884–1958) became the first professor of economics at the Netherlands School of Economics (Rotterdam), which was founded in 1913. In 1945 he accepted an offer of the University of Amsterdam to teach economics in its Faculty of Law. On the occasion of his 70th birthday, May 2, 1954, his pupils created the Prof. F. de Vries Foundation to honour a most influential teacher and a scholar of outstanding theoretical and practical wisdom.

The aim of the foundation is regularly to invite prominent economists from abroad for a series of lectures on theoretical subjects, as a stimulus to theoretical work in economics in the Netherlands.

INTRODUCTION

Professor Peter John de la Fosse Wiles was born on 25 November 1919 and served with the Royal Artillery during 1940-1945. He became fellow of All Souls College (Oxford) 1947/48 and of New College from 1948 to 1960. From 1960 to 1963 he was Professor at Brandeis University in the United States and was research fellow at Professor Gunnar Myrdal's Institut för internationell ekonomi, Stockholm, 1963/64. He had already been visiting professor at Columbia University in 1958 and acted in that capacity at the City College of New York in 1964 and 1967.

Among his publications are *The Political Economy of Communism* (1962), *Price, Cost and Output* of the same year, and *Communist International Economics* (1968).

It was in particular his deep-digging work "Income Distribution under Communism and Capitalism" (together with S. Markowski), published in *Soviet Studies* 1970/71 (p. 344ff, and p. 487ff) which induced the Board of the F. de Vries Foundation to invite Professor Wiles to deliver the F. de Vries lectures, which took place on November 8 and 9, 1973 at the Netherlands School of Economics (after February 1, 1974 the Economics Faculty of the Erasmus University in Rotterdam). In his lectures Professor Wiles, in his challenging way, further contributed to this highly topical subject.

J. Tinbergen

FOREWORD

1. Even the North-Holland Publishing Company cannot manufacture a book as quickly as its author can have second thoughts. First, then a word of gratitude to them for their efficiency and tolerance, and to the F. de Vries Foundation for both the honour bestowed and the provocation inflicted. Thoughts are idle and unsystematic until they have to be delivered in large lecture halls before critical audiences.

2. Since delivering these lectures I have been in harmonious disagreement with Amartya Sen: just the kind of economist I am not, but with enough patience and kindness to be the perfect counterfoil. It is not, then, simply that the Gini coefficient is insensitive to extremes, uncertain in its reaction at all times, and a mere average where averaging is least appropriate (Lecture I). It is not simply that algebra is a plaything while arithmetic is for serious policy-makers (whose distant servant I consider myself to be). It is nice to sum up these two points by saying that there is no substitute for the full arithmetical array, and that those who think otherwise are seeking a philosophers' stone. But that is not all. By concentrating on the decile and if possible semi-decile ratio I see now that I am drawing attention to a radical cleavage in the tasks of those who study distribution.

The extremes are a matter of social policy and distributive justice, and this is what concerns Sen and me in our different ways. We both think, nearly everybody thinks, that they should be brought closer together. The decile ratio comes perhaps too far away from the extremes. If the data were available I would always take the *average* of the top centile (which gives explicit weight to millionaires) ÷ the *average* of the bottom decile (which includes all the old, unemployed and sick we need worry about)[1]. The semi-decile ratio is merely our best approximation to that. It follows that one of the most despised (and simple!) of all measures of inequality, the "range" or (the highest income - the lowest) ÷ the mean, which is described by Sen as "more or less a non-starter"[2] is one of the best. Alone among the indices commonly discussed, it points us in the right direction.[3]

But the distribution in the middle, which I wrongly call uninteresting, raises questions of anything but distributive justice. We are here in the area of justice in exchange, or catallactic justice to use the old and sorely missed term. *Customary* relativities, *competitive* prices, prices that genuinely cover all *costs*, marginal *productivities*, *trade-union* leap-frogging: this is neither the language of distributive justice nor that of equality.

All these middle ratios are a complicated anthropological matter, mainly concerned with the wages, farm prices and

[1] Perhaps the first people to recommend partial averages were O. Eltetö and E. Frigyes, in *Econometrica* April 1968.

[2] Sen 1973, pp. 23, 31.

[3] It is very similar to Stark's "low/high" percentage (Stark 1972, pp. 41-51): this is the percentage of "income units" above or below certain extreme values. It is no accident that Stark, like me, is an arithmetic man, not an algebra man. I.e. he is policy-oriented.

retailers' margins of individuals, not with family incomes. Get them wrong and you will have cost inflation (you'll probably have it anyway). It is often good policy – i.e. it keeps the savages quiet – to re-establish *in*equality. This is, for instance, the case with British miners. They have always earned more (underground) than other male (let alone female) workers; but there will be no peace until they earn "more more".

No arithmetical array, no algebraical formula, helps us here. We need techniques for following the fates of individuals and small groups: we need to know *who* is gaining on *whom*, not merely how anonymous statistical units are spread out. Distributive justice on the other hand is very much less complicated. It only asks *how much* people get, never mind why or how or who; and condemns certain ratios as too great. A society that relies on both the market and capitalism is so riveted by the problems of catallactic justice as never to raise its eyes to this other problem. Yet at the extremes catallactic justice (and injustice) in a market creates ratios we find distributively intolerable; and a concern for the one must yield, over a few centiles, to a concern for the other. This is the misty borderland explored in Lecture IV. But on what to do about trade unions, or the vast middle jungle between say, the 100th and the 10th centiles, I have here no more wisdom to offer than any more orthodox student of distribution.

3. Finally on theory, my crude arithmetical ratios and my insistence on looking at the whole array enable us to *banish welfare economics from the process of measurement*, and to restore the strictest objectivity to our actual measures. We concentrate on this or that ratio according to our welfare predilections (Lecture I/1) but the ratios themselves are quite deadpan. I am thus able to reject the very common view that nearly all statements about inequality are ethical, e.g.:

> "This methodological point essentially reflects the dual nature of our conception of inequality. There is, obviously, an objective element in this notion; a fifty-fifty division of a cake between two persons is clearly more equal in some straightforward sense than giving all to one and none to the other. On the other hand, in some complex problems of comparing alternative income distributions among a large number of people, it becomes very difficult to speak of inequality in a purely objective way, and the measurement of the inequality level could be intractable without bringing in some ethical concepts." (Sen 1973, p.3).

On the contrary, ethics only intrudes if we insist on a single mystical formula. Ethics is brought in by weighting. My measures do not weight, they simply count. They are *all* as simple as eating Sen's cake.

4. The omission of capital gains needs longer defence than it got in the text. On whatever basis they are taxed, and whatever ideas anyone may have of fairness, capital values must of course be deflated before capital gains (which are normally reckoned by historical accountancy) constitute income for comparable purposes. Now one year differs greatly from another, but from 1962 to 1969, i.e. in the seven years before our chosen British year, realized plus unrealized capital gains were really about £1000 mn a year.[1] About 58% of them accrued to the top semi-decile. This is the average ratio in

[1] Estimated net wealth of individuals according to the Inland Revenue for 1969 minus net personal saving each year, plus capital taxes, all duly inflated, minus wealth in 1962. Workings available on request. Corporate ploughback is excluded from savings, i.e. its effect on capital values is called a capital gain.

1959 and 1962, using historical accountancy,[1] or £580 mn. This is 15.2% of the other income of this group, while the rest of the population got 2.4% from this source. This indicates very approximately that we should raise the British semidecile ratio by 10% if this item is to be included (bear in mind that the 96th centile must have had far smaller gains than the 100th).

But small unrealized capital gains do not, I make bold to say, constitute increasing command over resources. We can hardly say, as Stark suggests, that they "*may* cause changes in consumption or savings plans by directly influencing 'liquidity' preference, expectations and uncertainty. These effects *could perhaps* lead to a reduction in the holdings of 'liquid' or safe assets or an increase in the consumption of consumer durables or other forms of non-monetary assets".[2] I do not think this is true except of large unrealized capital gains in the top centile. But this stratosphere is beyond our ken, and we have already said flatly that the centile ratio must be much higher in U.K. than in USSR.

I therefore stick to my opinion that only realized capital gains count below the top centile. These are of course trivial.[3] This being so, corporate ploughback must only count when realized as a capital gain (so trivial) or in a dividend (already in our definition of income).

5. Further study of the Soviet data leads to the warning that in 1946 real inequality was smaller than indicated. Until 16th September 1946 bread (then the largest single item in the budget) was rationed at a very low price: i.e. the social cost of

[1] My workings (available on request) on the basis of Stark 1972 pp. 34,76.

[2] Stark 1973 pp. 20-21. My italics.

[3] Wiles and Markowski 1971, pp. 359, 361.

living index (Lecture I/1) was very "pro-poor". On that day bread was de-rationed and its price was raised; but wages were raised by a scale ranging from R 110 p.a. at the bottom to R 80 in the top class but one, and nothing for the richest (Wiles 1953 p. 337). This implies no less than the doubling of the lowest wages. We thus find a traumatic division of the year we are forced to rely upon into two statistically very different periods. But in the earlier prices are very "pro-poor" and in the later money incomes are much more equal than the annual average. So - if Loznevaya's figures mean what they say - inequality was overstated in both periods.

6. Further work, still very preliminary and inaccurate, enables me to add to "Our Grand Results" in Table VIII Lecture II. The Swedish semi-decile ratio is 3, the Danish 6, the Canadian 12, each after income-tax. So my concentration on the "range" has not lost its capacity to surprise! Thus Sweden is more equal than Bulgaria, and a world-beater up to this point.[1]

[1] These workings are *not* yet available on request!

CONTENTS

THE DISTRIBUTION OF WAGES PER EARNER AND OF INCOME PER HEAD IN THE U.S.S.R. *

1. The Soviet literature on this subject is vast and sophisticated. There are many good – and some not so good – writers, they have developed formulae and concepts as useful and original as in any other country. They clearly dispose of innumerable surveys and a rich store of data, but scarcely any absolute figure has ever been published. All numerical data are drawn from unspecified areas rather than the whole country, or are marked "stipulated" (*uslovni*). All diagrams are given without absolute numbers on the axes. Recently histograms have appeared where the horizontal axis is broken near the origin, so that even logarithmic distance is unascertainable (fig. 2).[1]

Meanwhile East European data are published in profusion. They show societies appreciably more equal than the U.K., or *a fortiori* the U.S.A. So it is clear that the Soviet authorities

* I owe a great deal to the help of Miss Helena Brus, Mrs. Linda Friedman and Messrs. Frank Srba and Andrew Threipland. Much of the literature was discovered by Mr. Mervyn Matthews.

[1] There are also figures for the average wage in this or that occupation.

are seeking to conceal from us an inequality greater than in Eastern and perhaps even than in Western Europe. This first lecture tries to unveil, or as I believe does unveil, the truth about the U.S.S.R. It is very boring. It contains no theory and no algebra, but only arithmetic. That is to say, it is about what is actually happening among a group of human beings – the supposed general object of economic study. But is may amuse you in a more vulgar way, since it is a detective story.

Before we proceed, a short word about concepts. First, I shall not hide my preference for equality. That is of course a value judgement. I do not think it affects my statistical workings. But I am also mainly interested in the rich and the poor, since it is upon them that any practical person must operate who wishes to achieve equality. The people between the quartiles do not interest me. So this second value judgement, *which is almost logically imposed by any commitment to equality,* does affect my choice of measures.

Secondly, my concepts are taken from the Soviet writers on income distribution because I think they are the best. We need to know wages per earner in order to study the labour market, and disposable family incomes per head in order to study welfare. Ideally these "heads" would be weighted according to need, i.e. approximately by age, sex and occupation. But the state of our data does not permit such refinement. [2] Mere family incomes, almost invariably used in Western studies, are virtually pointless and much understate inequality in all societies, since the poorest people come disproportionately from large families with moderately high incomes, and the richest from small families with not the highest incomes (cf. tables III and IV in Lecture II). And of course this discrepancy, which is

[2] For a Soviet and a British example cf. Wiles and Markowski 1971, p. 348.

sociological or demographic, varies from country to country.[3] Indeed I have no way of allowing for the effect on two societies, equally egalitarian in intention and fiscal arrangements, of a greater proportion of pensioners, divorcees or simply sick people in one of them.

The mention of sickness reminds us of the valuable but ill-defined notion of permanent income (Friedman 1957, pp. 25–30). Whatever its uses, this notion is almost irrelevant to distribution. For permanent incomes would only be more equally distributed than the observed over, say, one year if they tended to be greater below the median and smaller above it. But there is no reason to believe such a thing, except, say, at the lowest centile and the top millile. Thus, if the two richest families in a nation of 1000 families are equally rich, and their observed annual incomes fluctuate at random about a constant sum, and the 998th family is not "in the same class of money", the richest annual income will always exceed the richest permanent income. But already at the extreme centile this effect is lost, since no nation has only 100 families. The same applies at the bottom end, except that the approach to subsistence level curtails the distribution, reducing the fluctuations about permanent income. But the extreme centiles are still beyond our knowledge. I do not even think there is any systematic difference between Communism and capitalism in the proportion of permanent to observed income.

Among the flurry of innovations in our thinking on income

[3] Thus in the U.S.A. in 1968 the average size of family in the lowest per capita decile was 3.85, in the highest 2.00 (Wiles and Markowski 1971, table 9). But in the U.K. in 1969 the lowest was 4.55 and the highest 2.08 (Lecture II, table IV). True, these latter are households not families, but this is how the figures come to us. Then in Italy it is the other way round: 3.18 and 3.63 respectively (from my workings for table II/VIII).

distribution is the idea that we should use the market to level out the temporal incidence of life-time incomes, while leaving inter-life fluctuations to take care of themselves. For quite likely more year-by-year inequality is generated by intracycle than by inter-cycle inequality. This is not the same as the "permanent income" argument, since "permanent" is shorter than "life-time", and indeed has never been precisely defined.

I do not deny the argument as a piece of logic, but I do not think it should be more than a secondary guide in redistributive policy. True, intra-cycle inequality is peculiarly unjust and anti-social, condemning children and old people to suffering for the benefit of late teen-agers and the middle-aged. It discriminates in favour of the strong against the weak. It is certain too that this is a right-wing view, which would render us more tolerant of the inheritance of capital and of a market-determined wage distribution – things that only bring about inter-cycle inequality. And that is not an argument against taking this view.

It must be rejected, not for ideological or political reasons, but because its supporters are simply in error when they claim that minor market adjustments can correct intra-cycle inequality. The idea is that one offers people more perfect opportunities to save, borrow and to insure, and then sits back. Now this simply will not work, because:

(i) We all begin our lives at a trough in the cycle. Not even Miss Ayn Rand would impose on an embryo the duty to earn, save and insure so that immediately after birth it can claim compensating benefits, corresponding to its previous thrift, to tide it over the bad early years. Not even Confucius, who spent 60 years in the womb, was able to do that, though undoubtedly he would have appreciated the argument. As to borrowing, no bank would lend to a baby, not even Confucius. Parallel to "you can't take it with you" there is "you can't bring it with you" – not even if there is transmigration of souls. Thus we are born wholly dependent on a particular stage in our parents' life-cycles, and that too a poor one, so that justice and equality within generations depend on the same between generations, i.e. on inter-cycle equality.

(ii) It is much more reasonable to expect people to provide their own pensions, but here too we must take account, even if we are economists, of the nature of things. People get sick or make mistakes in middle life, wives are deserted, skills rendered obsolete, savings nullified by inflation. Only healthy people who are good with money and lucky in their lives can fairly be expected to provide the whole of an adequate pension. These are a minority among us.

We have no figures, but East Europe and the U.S.S.R. do not seem to have levelled out intra-cycle fluctuations much better than capitalism, since their social services and pensions are not all that bigger (below). Nay more, capitalism concentrates money in the hands of widows by inheritance, and thus by its very nature assures, in a very haphazard way, one element of intra-cycle equality.

I turn to the social cost of living index. This is an index for groups distinguished by income or demographic characteristics, taking the nation as 100, and confined to a single point of time. No such indices exist to my knowledge, though of course there are temporal indices for various social groups. This is another large lacuna in our knowledge of distribution. In the U.S.A. the index for the poor may well > 100, owing to high prices in slum shops (caused mainly by theft and other hazards). The sheer unavailability of luxuries makes this index very favourable to the poor under Communism. In the U.S.S.R. the index for the poor undoubtedly < 100, since children's clothing, black bread and urban transport bear little or no turnover tax. But the same undoubtedly applies to the very rich, who are powerful enough to acquire things otherwise unavailable, and have access to the secret privileged shops (*zakrytye raspredeliteli*). It is both these classes, furthermore, that seem to be the main beneficiaries of the ridiculously low state house rents (cooperative housing is common in between).

As to sheer accountancy, wages should, but often do not, include fringe benefits and expense accounts. Family income should, and usually does, include social services in money, income from capital, earnings from moonlighting, auto-consumption in kind and the imputed rents of owner-occupancy. These rents, however, are omitted by Communist statisticians. The main result must be that they understate the incomes of collective farmers. The collective social services in kind must, most unfortunately, be omitted from all comparisons, since we have so few and such bad data on their enjoyment by individuals. This is an inevitable defect in our estimates, particularly regrettable since such services weigh rather more under Communism.[4] Though perhaps rather less equally distributed than

[4] This is not an easy figure to work out, since the immense Soviet turnover tax is not levied on most of the services directly supplied to consumers by the State (S). Indirect support, or monetary benefits (B), and earned income of all sorts (E) bear the whole of this tax. I further note that profits are much greater in enterprises producing for the consumer market (one quarter of all industrial profit). We must therefore inflate S from factor cost to market price, thus (1969, md. R):

turnover tax 44.5[c];
enterprise profits in light and food industry 12.3[c];
private consumption 166.2[c];
material consumption by institutions directly serving the public 15.3[c];

$$\text{notional market price for } S\text{: } S\left(1 + \frac{44.5 + 6.1^{a}}{166.2 + 15.3}\right) = 1.28\,S.$$

Now $S + B = 0.34\,E^{b}$ and $S/B = 60^{b}/40$ at factor cost for S.
So $S/(S+B+E)$ at market prices = 18.7% [footnote continues].

the smaller volume of the same services under capitalism, their net effect must surely be greater equality of total consumption. Then the deduction of income-tax has been a major preoccupation, especially for Britain. Realized capital gains appear to be very small[5], while unrealized ones are best neglected until the later period when they are realized.[6] The same point applies to corporate ploughback; incidentally if we impute this to current capitalist income we must also impute it to workers in most reformed Communist systems, who stand to enjoy greater bonuses as a result of current ploughback.

2.I pay less heed to wages in these first two lectures since they are only a stepping-stone to per capita family income. It is no concern until later whether fringe benefits have been adequately treated. My basic question is: how unequal are likely to be any two people in a given society? But this raises the question of the formula for expressing degrees of inequality. All the accepted formulae are averages of differences[7]: the

In the U.K., where the difference between factor cost and market price is much less important, this ratio was about 10% in 1967 (workings available on request).

[a] Arbitrary: ½ of 12.3.

[b] Sarkisyan 1972, pp. 135–6.

[c] *Nar. Khoz.* 1969, pp. 559, 744, 769.

[5] Cf. Wiles and Markowski 1971, p. 359. In any case we have no figures for them by families.

[6] Here again we are forced to this choice by lack of data. But the "accruals" basis for reckoning income surely gives quite a false picture of how families, as opposed to corporations, act, and of what they consider to be saving. Moreover, if very rich people borrow on the strength of unrealized capital gains they must still repay.

[7] I assume without discussion that Pareto's is entirely unacceptable, since it only concerns the distribution above the mode. Moreover, the assumption of constant elasticity is totally without theoretical or intuitive content.

variance, the Gini coefficient, etc. But there can surely be no subject upon which an average, even an average of differences, throws less light than the inequality of the things being averaged! So my basic question is not: how unequal are likely to be any two *random* people – I understand, though no mathematican, that this is the question the Gini coefficient answers, but: how different are the rich and the poor?

We must not be fooled by the mere sophistication of this coefficient, and of the Lorenz curve on which it rests. Anyone who has actually worked with a Lorenz curve on real numbers will know that even on an inconveniently large scale, and with a thin pencil, which printers cannot cheaply reproduce, it still renders almost invisible the difference between an egalitarian and an inegalitarian society at the lower end. For if the income of an individual is the slope of the Lorenz curve above him, the slopes of small incomes cannot be visibly differentiated, even though the incomes differ a great deal.

Indeed it appears that under ordinary circumstances the Gini coefficient (and so also the coefficient of deviation, which is twice its value) is extremely insensitive to redistribution, at least between the extremes. Thus take the following distribution, which is somewhat more equal than that of the U.S.A. in Lecture II, table VIII, and has been simplified only in order to ease calculation:

Case I:

Persons	1, :	£30
	2, ..., 5:	£20
	6, ..., 15:	£15
	16, ..., 50:	£11
	51, ..., 85:	£ 7
	86, ..., 95:	£ 3.5
	96, ..., 100:	£ 2

Semi-decile ratio = 10
Gini coefficient = 0.253

We now perform a veritable social revolution, raising by 50% the income of the poor at the expense of the rich. This is about the most that might happen without violence, but certainly not without extreme political excitement:

Case II:

Persons 1	: £25	
2, ..., 5	: £19	
6, ..., 15	: £15	Semi-decile ratio = 6.33
16, ..., 50	: £11	Gini coefficient = 0.235
51, ..., 85	: £ 7	
86, ..., 95	: £ 3.9	
96, ..., 100	: £ 3	

The semi-decile ratio is cut by 37%, while the Gini coefficient falls by 7%. Now let us go in for red revolution (III). We confiscate all capitalist ownership, thus reducing the rich at the semi-decile ratio by 20%[8] relatively to Case I. Our fiscal re-arrangements are such as to double the income of the poor, add 50% to that of the lower proletariat, and take 7% from the fairly rich. This time the Gini coefficient falls by 27% – a dégringolade mainly due to the transfers between the two middle ranges:

[8] This is approximately right for the U.K.: cf. Wiles and Markowski 1971, p. 498. I make allowance for some confiscation also of mixed incomes, and for compensation of poor pensioners who were living on private capital. All this is more or less our Idealtypus D, or "Poland", in Lecture V.

Case III:

Persons 1	: £16	
2, ..., 5	: £16	
6, ..., 15	: £14	
16, ..., 50	: £11	Semi-decile ratio = 4
51, ..., 85	: £ 7.42	Gini coefficient = 0.185
86, ..., 95	: £ 5	
96, ..., 100	: £ 4	

Finally we can use these figures to warn against using the quartile ratio. For it is easy to equalize between the 16th and 85th centiles by deducting income at the bottom and adding it at the top:

Case IV:

Persons 1	: £30	
2, ..., 5	: £20.65	
6, ..., 15	: £15	
16, ..., 50	: £10.7	Semi-decile ratio = 11.0
51, ..., 85	: £ 7.5	Gini coefficient = 0.253
86, ..., 95	: £ 2.6	
96, ..., 100	: £ 1.88	

The quartile ratio, which was 1.57 in Case I, is now 1.43, moving in the opposite direction to the semi-decile ratio. The main redistribution will be seen as being from the very poor to the upper middle class, and there will be blood in the streets. Yet the Gini coefficient has not changed.

So I reject altogether the Gini coefficient as a serious measure of inequality, until its performance in various circumstances has been better explored *arithmetically*.[9] Ease of alge-

[9] For a similar but less sharp statement cf. Atkinson 1970. Mr.

braical handling should be not of secondary but of tertiary interest in a choice of formula, and the mere weight of tradition should count for zero.

Obviously a general index used to characterize an array, or a mathematical function used to describe an array, gains no objective validity whatever from its mathematical manoeuvreability. Pareto's Law is not true because it can be simply stated. Gini's coefficient is just an arbitrarily chosen average, as misleading as other averages. Anyone who attempts to contest this proposition is not a statistician but, to use no ruder word, a numerologist. The distribution of income in Britain above the mode might be Paretian this year, but that does not prove it was Paretian the year before. The same Gini coefficient can describe Lorenz curves that cross once, twice or more often. The coefficient can, as we have seen, hardly distinguish societies of radically different structure.

The Lorenz curve itself, however, *is* simply an array. It is an in practice incomprehensible way of showing the data, but it does show all the data. It does not average them, and it does not force them to conform to a mathematical formula. It simply makes them impossible to use, since it converts legible arithmetic into illegible geometry. So it is also in its own way the plaything of the theoretician, not the tool of the practical man. Indeed some writers, recognizing the insensitivity of the Gini coefficient, have begun to specify the slope of the Lorenz curve at various points in an accompanying diagram. I.e. they list the incomes at various quantiles, but not in rubles or £ but only in proportions to the average! Such a concession to real-

Atkinson unfortunately operates without arithmetical examples, and so cannot quantify the defects of this coefficient. I owe a great deal to discussion with Amartya Sen.

ity is extremely destructive of the high mathematical tradition while doing obeisance to its forms.

Therefore I accept the simpler and easier to see (and cheaper to print!) Soviet technique of listing the semi-decile, decile and quartile ratios. After all, the visiting economist does not see the Gini coefficient as he walks about the down-town and the slums of a foreign capital. Revolutionary agitators, and the depressed but resentful poor, and the politicians who debate distribution in parliament, and the rich who sleep with revolvers under their pillows, do not see it either. What we all see is the semi-decile ratio, or at any rate some such thing. So why don't we all just go ahead and measure it? The inequality of two incomes is the ratio that one has to another; it is not some incomprehensibly sophisticated average that reflects few of the changes that really concern ordinary people. If the inequality of many incomes has to be many such ratios, well that is how the world is constructed. Elegance, unity and simplicity are *graces* with which good fortune may or may not crown our intellectual achievements, they lend those achievements no sort of authority.

It would be nice, indeed it would be a very great improvement, to add the centile and millile ratios, or some such ratio as $P_{99.9}/P_5$. But we cannot do so, since our data are not good enough. Indeed my general conclusion that Soviet society is as unequal as British society will surely not hold at all at millile level. Try, incidentally, to show the millile ratio on a Lorenz curve!

3. With the publication of Rabkina and Rimashevskaya (1972), hereafter called "R. and R.", it is possible to say very much more about wage distribution per earner and income

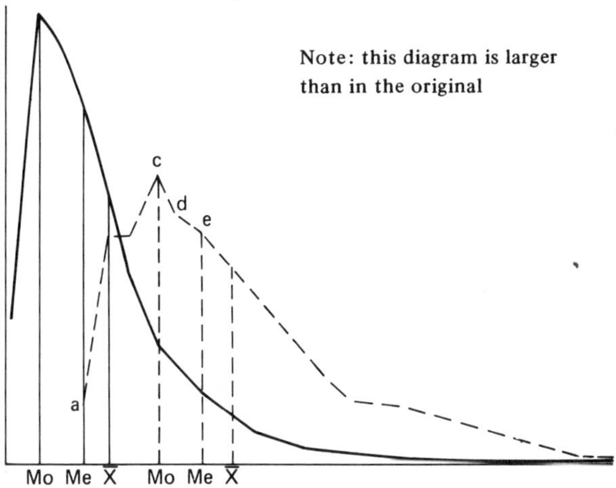

Fig. 1. Distribution of workers and employees in socialized sector of the U.S.S.R. by individual earnings, 1946 and 1966.

distribution per head.[10] The authors have not been allowed to publish one single fact directly: as usual not one diagram has any numbers written along the axes; all the tables have numbers but each one is only "stipulated". But we have quite enough to go on, in combination with the previous article of Loznevaya (1968), to restore the numbers that the censors rubbed out.

We start with the distribution of wages and salaries among "workers and employees of the national economy", i.e. the whole socialist sector, in 1966. Loznevaya gives a diagram that we here reproduce as fig. 1.

R. and R. give the one that we reproduce as fig. 2.

[10] But cf. Pryor 1972: a similar article, with similar results. For a recent book on Soviet wage-setting see Kirsch 1972.

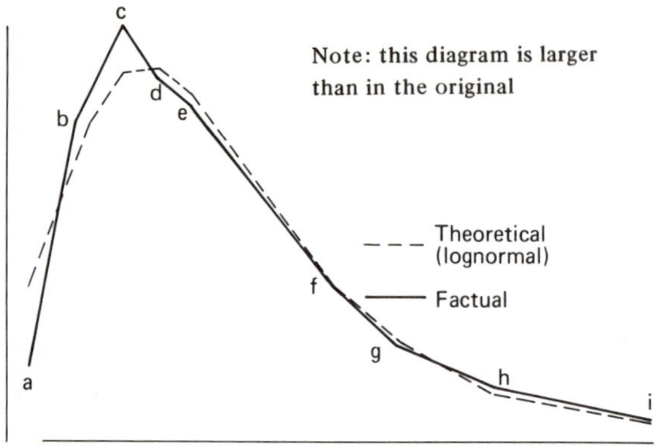

Fig. 2.

R. and R. seem to have smoothed Loznevaya's figure at the points *b* (where an interval has been suppressed), and *g*/*h*. But essentially it is the same figure. Thus the vertical and horizontal distances *ac, ad, ae* all bear the relation 2.5:4 approx. (Loznevaya: R. and R.).

But R. and R. have displaced the whole figure towards the vertical axis, so as to make it impossible to measure the number of rubles represented by *a*, and so by any other point. They have done this systematically in every figure in their book, and have honestly indicated as much by breaking the abscissa before it meets the ordinate. On the other hand, the vertical distances of points *a, c, d* and *e* from the abscissa are all 4/2.5 times those in Loznevaya, like the vertical distances between points. So there has been no shift here.

However, all this labour of concealment is in vain, since Loznevaya not only showed the origin in the appropriate horizontal relation to *a* (i.e. as a number of rubles), but also gave us other clues as to the deleted numbers on her ordinate and abscissa. I quote what Markowski and I wrote in 1971, with a few inconsequential amendments (pp. 501–4):

"Thus Loznevaya give us these relationships between horizontal distances, where 4 and 6 subscript mean 1946 and 1966:

$X_6 = 2.2\ X_4$, where X is the mean wage
$Me_6 = 2.5\ Me_4$, where Me is the median wage
$Mo_6 = 3.9\ Mo_4$, where Mo is the modal wage
$Mo_4 = 0.380\ X_4 = 0.498\ Me_4$
$Mo_6 = 0.674\ X_6 = 0.769\ Me_6$
$Me_4 = 0.762\ X_4$. Top $decile_4 = 7.24 \times$ bottom $decile_4$
$Me_6 = 0.897\ X_6$. Top $decile_6 = 3.26 \times$ bottom $decile_6$
$= 1.8 \times$ top $decile_4$
Bottom $decile_6 = 4 \times$ bottom $decile_4$

These horizontal relations all correspond within 1% to those obtainable by measuring the absolute distances in the figure. Moreover, the figure itself has been ill printed or deliberately distorted. The vertical lines are not quite parallel to each other, and none of them is exactly at right angles to the horizontal.

"On vertical distances, Loznevaya says that the percentage of earners in each income group rose (+) or fell (–) 'by the following multiple in the 20 years'.[11] Her twelve multiples are set out, unchanged, in col. 3 of Table I, opposite the ruble intervals she gives (col. 2). We take the multiples to mean that the percentage of earners in the R40–50 bracket in 1966 was 1.2 times as great as in 1946, and that in the R50–60 bracket the percentage in 1946 was 1.2 times as great as in 1966, etc. Note only the group R0–30: Loznevaya's figure is clearly a

[11] 'V opredelennoe chislo raz za 20 let.'

TABLE 1

SOVIET WAGES AND SALARIES, 1946 AND 1966 (FROM LOZNEVAYA)

Corres-ponding points in fig. 1	Distance of kink [a] from ordinate (mm.)	Income bracket in rubles per month	Loznevaya's multiples, 1966/1946	Height of bracket mid-points (mm.)		Approximate percentages per actual interval	
				1946	1966	1946	1966
	(1)	(2)	(3)	(4)	(5)	(6)	(7)
	1.1	0–10		15.1	0	6.0	0
	4.4 (mode)	10–20	–3.2 [b]	46.7	0	18.7	0
	6.5	20–30		*c* 43	0	17.2	0
a	8.6	30–40	–7.3	39.0	5.4	15.6	2.1
	11.1	40–50	–1.2	28.7	23.4	11.4	8.8
	13.8	50–60	+1.2	19.9	23.5	8.0	8.8
c	17.5 (mode)	60–70	+2.4	12.7	30.2	5.1	11.3
d	19.1	70–80		10.3	26.2	4.1	9.8
	23.4 [c]	80–100	+3.5	6.4	22.3	5.0	16.7
	27.0	100–120	+4.9	3.7	18.2	3.0	13.7
	32.1 [c]	120–140	+6.0	*c* 2.1 [d]	12.7	1.6	9.6
	38.2	140–160	+5.6	*c* 1.2 [d]	6.6	1.0	5.0
	46.9	160–200	+5.3	*c* 1.2 [d]	6.4	2.0	9.6
	63.6	200–300	+4.3	*c* 0.3 [d]	1.6 [e]	1.0	5.5
	–	300 +	+3.3				
	Total			250.0 [f]	269.9 [f]	99.7	100.9

[a] Or beginning of line, or assumed mid-point where there is no obvious kink in either line.

[b] This multiple we have perforce rejected.

[c] No obvious kink: the point *e* seems to be at R85, or in the middle of R80–90.

[d] Derived by using the multiple: direct measurement impossible.

[e] See text below.

[f] Counting each figure once for each R10 it represents.

misprint, possibly for –32.0. She shows, in fact, no one at all in this group in 1966.

"We infer from this table, from the position of the kinks in the figure, and from the income intervals for which Loznevaya gives multiples, that the same intervals were used for both distributions. We further assume – and it is a very vital assumption – that the kinks represent mid-points in these intervals, except that the kinks at the modes might represent the actual values of the modes. It is now easy to reconstruct the whole original figure. We reason as follows. The multiples show that the cross-over point of the two curves is about R50. Therefore, the interval mid-points can be accommodated to the kinks as cols. 1 and 2 of Table I. Note the overwhelmingly plausible character of the ruble intervals yielded by the initial assumption. This is the strongest proof that we have 'cracked the code'.

"The figure proves amazingly accurate. At every kink the heights are genuinely and without forcing related to each other by the given multiple in col. 3. We have only used the multiple to manipulate the results where there is no visible kink. Judging by the larger distances, which are more accurate, 2.5 mm. are R10. It follows that R15 is 3.75 mm., and Mo_4 lies between R15 and R20, while the figure treats it as a mid-point. The presentation of Mo_6 is similarly inaccurate, since 17.5 mm. is well above the interval mid-point of 16.3 mm (R65). The other kinks seem to be all genuine mid-points. Measuring off on the figure, we obtain:

	rubles unadjusted	rubles adjusted
Mo_4 = 4.4 mm. =	17.6	17.6
Me_4 = 8.7 mm. =	34.8	35.0
X_4 = 11.4 mm. =	45.6	46.0
Mo_6 = 17.5 mm. =	70.0	68.5
Me_6 = 22.3 mm. =	89.2	89.2
X_6 = 25.4 mm. =	101.6	101.6

The 'adjusted' column is the best I can do to allow for the relations Loznevaya asserts to hold between the magnitudes. This column also corresponds within 3% to the only two facts known otherwise: X_4 = R47.5, X_6 = R99.2.[12] It would be nice if this latter correspondence were better: rounding error will not explain 3%. However, such differences between national averages and the averages of surveys are commonplace in other countries.

"The totals are so calculated as to weight a vertical distance more, the greater the horizontal distance it represents. So although they are expressed in mm. vertically they are good proxies for the total area under each curve, or 100%. Putting each of these unfortunately discrepant totals in (4) and (5) at 100%, we arrive at cols. 6 and 7.

"We must now check these results as best we can. We know, first, both medians, so we know that the frequencies represented by the curves to their left add up to 50%. The added heights of all the mid-points below the medians are 125 mm. in 1946 and 130 mm. in 1966. So the upper medians are 125 (correct) and 139.9 (incorrect) respectively. However, with the help of our knowledge of the decile coefficients we can obtain some reassurance. The bottom deciles are obtainable with less guesswork, and we may compare the top deciles obtained from our table with their values as implied by the decile ratios given:

bottom decile_4 = c. R12.5; top decile_4 from table I = c. R90, by using the ratio c. R90.5;

[12] *Narodnoye Khozyaistvo SSSR v 1967 g.*, Moscow 1967, p. 657. The 1969 yearbook (p. 539) has 48.1 and R100.2. I let the text stand because it gives the data available to Loznevaya when she was writing, and I assume she checked her average against the current yearbook.

bottom $decile_6$ = c. R50.0; top $decile_6$ from table I = c. R173,
by using the ratio c. R163;
R12.5 X 4 = R50 (correct); R90 X 1.28 = R162 (correct?).

"So far with virtually no manipulation: we have rejected one very obvious error, and we have allowed that the thickness of the line can interfere with close measurement. To manipulate further, in order to obtain consistency, would be the serious crime of lèse-data. But we have used up all our resources except to check the means by multiplying out. X_4 comes out at R48.8 and X_6 at R107.0 – errors of 3% and 8%."

4. Lest all this working seem hypothetical, we can now confirm it from R. and R. to the hilt. In doing so we use precisely one of Loznevaya's many absolute data. First, here are the horizontal distances between the points in R. and R.'s 1966 (in mm.):

a–b 6; *b–c* 6; *c–d* 4; *d–e* 4; *e–f* 18; *f–g* 8; *g–h* 12.

We can now deduce the breadth of the income bracket about each point as follows. We know that the points are all midpoints (R. and R. pp. 133–4). Now *d* stands midway between *c* and *e*, so its own bracket probably extends 2 mm. to either side. But then *e*'s brackets must do the same with respect to *e*. Then *b*'s bracket begins at a distance of 4 mm. away towards *c*, and so is 8 mm. broad. 4 mm. begins to look like R10; indeed it must in any case, if R10 = 2.5 mm. in fig. 1.

Now suppose the line between *f* and *g* lies midway between them; then they each have 8 mm. (R20) brackets. Then *h* has a 16 mm. bracket. Moreover there must be points between *e* and *f* that left no visible cusp or inflection. Of the intervening 18 mm. *e*'s bracket takes up two, and *f*'s four. That leaves

TABLE II

TABLE I REVISED, USING R. AND R. (1966 ONLY)

Inferred ruble intervals	Point in fig. 2	Height (mm)	Population (%)	Further interpolation [d] R	%
< 40 [f]	*a*	8.7	? 2.1 [b]		
40–60	*b*	38.1	18.7	(40–50 (50–60	7.9? 10.8?
60–70	*c*	49.2	12.1		
70–80	*d*	43.1	10.5		
80–90	*e*	39.5	9.7		
90–100	(*x*)	34.9	8.5		
100–120	(*y*)	28.0	13.7	(100–110 (110–120	7.5? 6.2?
120–140	*f*	18.6	9.1	(120–130 (130–140	5.1? 4.0?
140–160	*g*	11.4	5.6	(140–150 (150–160	3.2? 2.4?
160–200	*h*	6.5	6.4		
200–260 [c]	*i*	2.5	3.6		
> 260	–	–	? 0.6[a]		
		407.6 [e] (=99.8%)	100.2		

[a] Guessed: see text.
[b] Derived from Loznevaya: see table I.
[c] Uncertain: see text.
[d] Unfortunately necessary for our further workings: see table III.
[e] Counting each figure once for each R10 it represents.
[f] Assumed to represent R30–40 only: it should be borne in mind that R45 was the official minimum wage.

12 mm., most probably a bracket of 4 mm. (*x*), and one of 8 mm. (*y*).

Now *c* is the mode, and Loznevaya's mode was in the R60–70 bracket (R68.5, after adjustment). We therefore tentatively assign our points to the ruble brackets shown in table II. The fit is very perfect because these are more or less the ruble brackets actually used by R. and R. in their stipulated (*uslovni*) arithmetical examples:

<50, 50–60, 60–70, 70–80, 80–90, 90–100, 100–120, 120–140, 140–160, 160–200, >200 (pp. 73, 185, 190);
Ditto, but 40–50 for <50, 200–240 for >200 (p. 169);
<60, 60–70, 70–80, 80–90, 90–100, 100–120, 120–140, 140–160, 160–200, 200–240, 240–280, >280. (pp. 223, 230, 240)

Once we recognise that *c* is R60–70 and *h* is R160–200 we are forced to accept 4 mm. = R10, and all the other intervals follow as shown in table II.

We shall in general prefer R. and R.'s figure, *even though* Loznevaya's is more irregular and improbable. The smoothing out of her two intervals R40–50 and R50–60 into the single point *b* is especially suspicious. As the classicists say, *difficilior lectio potior.* But her figure is very ill printed on the right, and here we *must* use R. and R.'s larger scale and clearer print. They put *i* at a height of 3 mm., and if we take seriously the fact that *i* is at R230, it represents the mid-point of the bracket R200–260. So it is not an open-ended group, and it is on the basis of this inference that I have constructed table II. I have guessed those above R260 as shown.

Then, as Markowski and I made clear, Loznevaya's upper decile as derived from her ratios (R163) is virtually incompatible with our reconstruction of her graph (R173). Table II presents no such difficulty, since R. and R.'s graph also yields about R163.

We saw in fig. 1 and table I that Mo_4 contains 18.7% of the population, and that they earned between R10 and R20 and are 46.7 mm. high. But $46.7 \div 18.7 = 2.5$, so 1% of the population at R10 width is 2.5 mm. high. So the vertical unit has a convenient similarity to the horizontal unit, which we found to be R10 = 2.5 mm. So 1% = 2.5 $mm.^2$, in whatever shape. Similarly we find from fig. 2 and table II that the modal rectangle is 485 mm. high and 4 mm. broad, where R10 = 4 mm. But it contains 11.8% of the population, and $485 \div 11.8 \triangleq 4$, so 1% of the population at R10 width is 4 mm. high, and 1% is now 4 $mm.^2$.

So in both figures the height of 1% on a R10 bracket is the same as the breadth of R10: a coincidence too astounding not to be overwhelming confirmation of our estimates. The total population for 1946 in table I is exactly 250 mm. at R10 intervals, implying $2.5^2 \times 100$ $mm.^2$; and the 1966 total in table II is 407.6 at R10 intervals, implying $4^2 \times 100$ $mm.^2$ with an error of 2%. Loznevaya's error in 1966 is therefore 8% [(269.9–250)/250], and we find further reason to prefer R. and R. It is also clear that we have not much room for people above R260, since we have already 2% too much population (407.6 is 102% of the required 400). But if Loznevaya had a multiple for those above R300 already in 1946, this cannot have been a null class in 1966. The group > R260 can only be guessed, and I do so thus. Accept Loznevaya's implied deciles of R50 and R163. R161-3 contain about 0.6% of the population, so these must be added in again above R260.

As to the lowest group, we are happily assured of its population by the use of Loznevaya's multiple (table I). That is, we can derive this open-ended group from a group in 1946, which is not open-ended. The value of the group R40-50 is deduced from our acceptance of Loznevaya's lower decile as R50.

From all this, Table II results. The average wage comes out at R100.1, which is 1% off the officially published figure of R99.2 (above), and a great improvement on Loznevaya's R107.0 (above).

5. Next, R. and R. present on p. 215 an extremely useful array of purely empirical multipliers for converting deciles of pay per earner into deciles of family income per head. These ratios decline between 1958 and 1967 as shown, and I present by interpolation a set for 1966 in table III. The language of R. and R. is unambiguous, and I have surely not misused their multipliers: "Thus the fraction that results from dividing each decile or quartile of the distribution of labour earnings by the corresponding decile or quartile of the distribution of incomes represents a magnitude that notably declines with time. In confirmation we can adduce the following co-efficients, calculated from the materials of a sample survey of the incomes of workers' and employees' families in 1958 and 1967" (p. 214). Column 4, then, is our Holy Grail, or what the censors apparently wished to conceal; the distribution of non-peasant money incomes per head of population in the U.S.S.R. as a whole in 1966, before income-tax. Columns 5–7 are merely confirmatory. This yields, for family income per head, a decile ratio of 3.6, and a quartile of 2.0. We may plausibly add a semi-decile of about 6.0 from Appx. I table VIII, allowing for further equalization over time.

These are not even British standards of inequality (second lecture), and yet they exclude kolkhozniki. So we have still an underestimate (Lecture III).

Since then Eastern Europe is more equal, including its peasantry, than the U.S.S.R. without it (Lecture II), we can hardly wonder at the Soviet embarrassment which inhibits publication. The Soviet authorities may to a small extent console themselves with the vast regional differences with which they have to cope (Lecture III). But the legacy of Stalin, made abundantly clear by Loznevaya (fig. 1), is a hard one to overcome.

TABLE III

THE DISTRIBUTION OF DISPOSABLE FAMILY INCOME IN THE U.S.S.R.

1	2	3			4	5	6	7
					Rubles of family income per head per month			
Deciles	Rubles of pay per earner[b] 1966	R. and R.'s multipliers			(2) ÷ (3)	Korzhenevski's region, c1963[c]	Raitsin's figure, c 1967[d]	Raitsin's oblast' 1958[e]
		(1958)	1966	(1967)				
I	50.0	2.09	1.90	1.88	26.3	37.4	32.6	27.3
II	59.2	1.95	1.71	1.68	34.6	43.8	39.1	37.5
III	67.6	1.90	1.67	1.64	40.5	49.1	47.8	42.5
IV	76.4	1.89	1.64	1.61	46.6	56.0	56.7	48.0
V	86.8[a]	1.86	1.63	1.60	53.2	63.9	66.7	53.6
VI	98.1	1.85	1.63	1.60	60.1	73.1	77.6	59.8
VII	111.4	1.88	1.64	1.61	67.9	84.0	89.1	66.3
VIII	130.5	1.78	1.61	1.59	81.1	98.3	102.3	77.5
IX	163.0	1.85	1.65	1.63	98.5	122.5	122.6	105.0

[a] Note that Loznevaya puts the median at R85.0.
[b] Interpolated from table II.
[c] Appx. I Table VI.
[d] Appx. I Table VIII.
[e] Appx. I Table IX.

TABLE IV
DECILE RATIOS

Year	Earnings of workers and employees	Family incomes per head
1928	3.82 [e]	
1934	4.15 [e]	
1946	7.24 [a]	
1956	4.4 [b]	? 5.0 [d]
1964	3.7 [b]	
1966	3.2 [b]/3.26 [a]	3.7 [c]
1968	2.7 [b]	
1970	3.2 [b]	

[a] Loznevaya, above.
[b] Sarkisyan, 1972, pp. 125, 126, 132.
[c] Table III.
[d] Extrapolated from table III (4.4 × 2.15 ÷ 1.90).
[e] Bergson 1946, p. 128.

However, if we view it dynamically in table IV the statistical record since Stalin is a very good one indeed. I doubt if any other country can show a more rapid and sweeping progress towards equality.

In all these tables, we have no more exact definition of income applicable to all sources, but it appears to include the produce of private allotments, miscellaneous earnings, social services other than education and medicine, and deposit interest; but to exclude owner-occupied rents.

LECTURE II

RECENT BRITISH INCOME DISTRIBUTION

1. We now turn to the British statistics, at boring length: you may wish to take me at my word and skip to Table VIII. You might suppose that, back now in civilization, we have no problems; a telephone call will produce the required elucidation of any apparent obscurity. This is not true at all: calls are transferred to other extensions, data are stored on incompatible computers, there were until recently no official figures for regional income, there is no social cost of living index, the data do not give income per head, etc. etc. Nevertheless, the U.K. probably has as many and as accurate data on distribution as any country.

These statistics are purely "for the record". They make every possible claim to objectivity, and none at all to explain anything or to suggest what ought to be done. Their conclusion is that incomes were probably slightly more unequally distributed in the U.K. in 1969 than in 1953–4. Their vain hope is to lay controversy on this matter, which has been acute, to rest. After 1969, of course, equalization has been rapid.

They resemble closely previous work in the same tradition.[1] I reject all evidence based on income-tax returns, in

[1] See page 28.

contrast to survey data that include the income-tax, as falsified; and I reject the Anglo-Scandinavian claim to a morality so superior that falsification is minor. But in any case the tax rests on fiscal, not sociological or economic, definitions of what is an income unit, and these units are not families or households, but something smaller.[2] There is no logic in the use of such a unit, and since the law differs from country to country it is useless for international comparisons. It is at most usable in temporal comparisons above the median, in one country, in a period when the law does not change.

It would have been easy to present the official sample surveys in a more comparable and informative lay-out. I hope that the many complaints and dangerous interpolations will indicate to responsible parties how they can improve the presentation of this priceless source. The world is moving into a period of maximum interest in this subject, with minimally comparable and minimally reliable data. We are almost never told family income per head in Western sources, and distributions are quite usually published without deciles or even averages. It is not too much to ask that the same professional attention be paid to this subject as to GNP.

[1] Wiles and Markowski 1971; Wiles, "Recent British and Communist Income Distribution", presented at the LSE conference, December 1971. This is a revised version of the latter paper; it comes to the opposite conclusion because the original data much understated the income tax in 1953–4.

[2] For a valiant attempt to defeat all these ogres cf. Stark 1972. I do not find the work convincing, but his general conclusions, at least, agree with mine. Incidentally Sweden, the paragon of the Western world, uses only income-tax based statistics for its study of income distribution. Swedish data are therefore quite incomparable with foreign data. The most I will admit is that income-tax data are useful for interpolation. They are so used, for instance, in my estimates of British regional inequality (Wiles 1974).

2. Tables I and II present the original data. The FES table for 1953–4 tells us so little that even a semi-decile ratio is unobtainable. Accordingly I use other data in the document (footnotes a and b to table I) to evolve columns of £20, £30 and £30+ and rows of 6 and 7+. The row and column totals being given, the breakdown in the matrix is rather strictly determined, and could not differ widely from the figures I have set down.

3. Tables III and IV shift these data to a per capita basis. Each group of figures sharing a common underlining will be recognised as a single figure in the "persons" column of tables I and II. The amount of interpolation is very great, but the reader may reassure himself as to the rather strict limits upon it by trying to move as few as 200 people (1%) from one column to the next in table III, the less accurate of the two. He will surely be unhappy with the results except in the neighbourhood of the median, where it does not matter anyway. Such unhappiness rests, however, on the basic assumption of all interpolation: *natura non facit saltum*. If smooth progression is not assumed our results are indeed arbitrary. See Appendix III.

4. The various quantile ratios result, alas, from further interpolation. First, the per capita figures are subdivided more finely, as in table V, and then they are interpolated by the method shown in Appendix I, table VI.

5. All these figures are gross of income tax and national insurance. The FES tells us (indirectly!) the incidence of income tax and national insurance on households of given incomes. This is by no means the same as data of incidence on households arranged in order of per capita income. For these

TABLE I

WEEKLY INCOMES AND SIZES OF HOUSEHOLDS, 1953–4 (F.E. S. 1953–4, p. 18.)

Persons per house-hold	> £50			£30–50			£20–30			£14–20			£10–14		
	hh [a]	pers	Yph	hh	pers	Yph	hh	pers	Yph	hh	pers	Yph	hh	pers	Yph
1	1	1	50+	3	3	30–50	5	5	20–30	20	20	14–20	60	60	10–14
2	12	24	25+	39	78	15–25	145	290	10–15	490	980	7–10	903	1806	5–7
3	17	51	16.67+	65	195	10–16.67	225	675	6.67–10	773	2319	4.67–6.67	1041	3123	3.33–4.67
4	19	76	12.5+	72	288	7.5–12.5	288	1152	5–7.5	621	2484	3.5–5	825	3300	2.5–3.5
5	14	70	10+	44	220	6–10	182	910	4–6	386	1930	2.8–4	360	1800	2–2.8
6+	15	–	–	48	–	–	220	–	–	288	–	–	236	–	–
6	7	42	8.33+	24	144	5–8.33	115	690	3.33–5	160	960	2.33–3.33	131	786	1.67–2.33
7+	8	60	7.14+	24	188	3.87–6.46	105	814	2.58–3.87	128	993	1.81–2.58	105	813	1.29–1.81
Total	78 [b]	324	–	271 [b]	1116	–	1065 [b]	4536	–	2578	9686	–	3425	11688	–

Table I (continued)

Persons per household	£8–10			£6–8			£3–6			⩾ £3			Total	
	hh	pers	Yph	hh	pers	Yph	hh	pers	Yph	hh	pers	Yph	hh	pers
1	94	94	8–10	151	151	6–8	337	337	3–6	635	635	< 3	1306	1306
2	651	1302	4–5	590	1180	3–4	721	1442	1.5–3	103	206	< 1.5	3654	7308
3	566	1698	2.67–3.33	388	1164	2–2.67	131	393	1–2	8	24	< 1	3214	9642
4	453	1812	2–2.5	194	776	1.5–2	57	228	0.75–1.5	1	4	< 0.75	2530	10120
5	183	915	1.4–20	73	365	1.2–1.4	27	135	0.6–1.2	–	–	–	1269	6345
6+	84	–	–	41	–	–	6	–	–	–	–	–	938	–
6	47	282	1.33–1.67	24	144	1–1.33	6	36	0.51	–	–	–	514 [c]	3084
7+	37	286	1.03–1.29	17	131	0.77–1.03	–	–	–	–	–	–	424 [c]	3285 [d]
Total	2031	6389	–	1437	3911	–	1279	2571	–	747	869	–	12911	41090

[a] "hh" = household, "pers." = persons, "Yph" = income per head.
[b] p. 19.
[c] p.12
[d] Residual: so the 7+ average is 7.75 per household.

TABLE II

WEEKLY INCOMES AND SIZE OF HOUSEHOLDS, 1969 (F.E.S. 1969, p. 78)[a]

Persons per household	£60+		£50–60		£40–50		£35–40		£30–35		£25–30	
	pers	Yph	pers	Yph	pers	Yph	pers	Yph	pers	Yph	pers	Yph
1	10	60+	10	50–60	24	40–50	18	35–40	27	30–35	50	25–30
2	220	30+	180	25–30	432	20–25	398	17.5–20	524	15–17.5	520	12.5–15
3	318	20+	333	16.67–20	714	13.33–16.67	507	11.67–13.33	603	10–11.67	657	8.33–10
4	540	15+	536	12.5 –15.0	872	10–12.5	708	8.75–10	820	7.5–8.75	708	6.25–7.5
5	365	12+	320	10–12	540	8–10	335	7–8	460	6–7	385	5–6
6	294	10+	210	8.33–10	282	6.67–8.33	156	5.83–6.67	168	5–5.83	222	4.17–5.0
7	126	8.5	105	7.14–8.57	168	5.71–7.14	105	5–5.71	49	4.29–5	77	3.57–4.29
8+	201	6.87+	96	5.73–6.87	87	4.58–5.73	96	4.01–4.8	131	3.44–4.01	113	2.86–3.44
Total people	2074		1790		3119		2323		2782		2732	

[a] Since this table contains no interpolation I have omitted the households columns, and gone straight to persons.

Table II (continued)

Persons per household	£20–25		£15–20		£10–15		£8–10		£6–8		>£6		Total
	pers	Yph	pers	Yph	pers	Yph	pers	Yph	pers	Yph	pers	Yph	pers
1	76	20–25	98	15–20	185	10–15	168	8–10	364	6–8	96	6	1126
2	584	10–12.5	512	7.5–10	708	5.0–7.5	254	4–5	30	3–4	16	3	4378
3	489	6.67–8.33	348	5.0–6.67	147	3.33–5	27	2.67–3.33	12	2.0–2.67	6	2	4161
4	524	5.0–6.25	244	3.75–5.0	100	2.5–3.75	4	2–2.5	12	1.5–2.0	16	1.5	5084
5	285	4–5	115	3.0–4.0	75	2–3	5	1.6–2.0	–	1.2–1.6	5	1.2	2890
6	120	3.3–4.17	66	2.5–3.33	30	1.67–2.5	6	1.33–1.67	6	1.0–1.33	–	1.0	1560
7	56	2.86–3.57	21	2.14–2.86	–	–	–	–	–	–	–	–	707
8+	79	2.29–2.86	35	1.72–2.29	–	–	–	–	–	–	–	–	838 [c]
Total people	2213		1439		1245		464		424		139		20744 [b]

[b] p.7.

[c] Residual. There were 96 households, so 8.75 persons on average.

TABLE III

TABLE I SHIFTED TO A "PER CAPITA" BASIS (PERSONS ONLY)

hh size	£10+	£9–10	£8–9	£7–8	£6–7	£5–6
1	89[a]	40	54	70	81	90
2	392	180	300	500	756	1050
3	246	72	171	339	93 + 429	1290
4	76 + 72	64	100	52 + 84	300	768
5	70		100 (← →)		120	295
6	12	30 (← →)		24 (← →)	30	90
7+	7		44 (← →)		9 + 16	30
Totals pers.	964		2224 (← →)		1834	3613
hh.	421		958		740	1315

[a] Households of one person are allocated thus at the top: £10–11, 27; £11–12, 17; £12–13, 10; £13–14, 6; £14–20, 20; £20–30, 5; £30–50, 3; £50+, 1. This makes the rest of the distribution more plausible, since it puts certain limitations on £9–10 etc.

[b] At the bottom we know from the figures for old age pensioners (pp. 246–7) that: there were 506 OAP households at under £3, and 307 above £3; 461 were one-person households; 318 two-person; 34 bigger; the one-person households averaged £2.80 expenditure and the two-person households £2.43. There is therefore a sharp peak in our £2–3 column.

Table III (continued)

hh size	£4–5	£3–4	£2–3	£1.5–2	£0–1.5	Total
1	110	137	400 [b]	170 [b]	65	1306
2	1302	1180	900 [b]	542 [b]	206	7308
3	600 + 1563	1560 + 999	699 + 1164	300	93 + 24	9642
4	1484	1000 + 1500	1800 + 1812	776	288 + 4	10120
5	615	1590	340 + 1800	765	150 + 365 + 135	6345
6	300	390 + 294	666 + 390	396 + 180	102 + 144 + 36	3084
7+	92	50 + 390	424 + 693	300 + 460	353 + 286 + 131	3285
Total	6066	9090	11088	3889	2322	41090
people	2037	2692	3118	1081	549	12911

Lower semi-decile = £1.43
Lower decile = £1.74

Lower quartile = £ 2.41
Median = £3.29
Upper quartile = £4.71
Upper decile = £6.40
Upper semi-decile = £8.26

TABLE IV

TABLE II SHIFTED TO A "PER CAPITA" BASIS

Persons per household	£25+	£24–25	£23–24	£22–23	£21–22	£20–21	£19–20	£18–19	£17–18	£16–17	£15–16
1	139	13	14	16	16	17	17	18	19	21	23
2	400	56	74	86	100	116	134	166	98 + 100	210	214
3	168	12	21	27	39	51	69	84	129	51 + 129	195
4	48	←		92		→	←		400		→
5	5	←		25		→	←		115		→
6	0	←		12		→	←		60		→
7	0	←		7		→	←		28		→
8+	0	←		9		→	←		18		→
Total pers.	760	←		803		→	←		2298		→
hh.	408	(£23–25, 113 households, 234 people)		374					917		

Lower semi-decile	£3.85	Upper quartile	£13.5
Lower decile	£4.71	Upper decile	£18.5
Lower quartile	£6.44	Upper semi-decile	£22.75
Median	£9.05		

Table IV (continued)

Persons per household	£14–15	£13–14	£12–13	£11–12	£10–11	£9–10	£8–9	£7–8
1	27	31	36	41	50	68	100	214
2	208	208	104 + 118	240	226	212	200	100 + 90
3	219	171 + 90	300	117 + 252	351	387	270 + 144	264
4	180	220	136 + 140	332	400	508	200 + 460	360 + 360
5	←	220	→	135	185	250	290	335
6	←		222		→	114	96 + 48	174
7	←		70			→	21 + 42	63 + 21
8+	←		51			→	44	63
Total pers.	←		6619			→	1915	2044
							599	693

Table IV (continued)

Persons per household	£6–7	£5–6	£4–5	£3–4	£2–3	£0–2	Total
1	150	50	25	12	6	3	1126
2	280	338	254	30	6	10	4378
3	81 + 147	201	108	39 + 15	12 + 12	6	4161
4	348 + 124	400	200	44 + 72	28 + 4	12 + 16	5084
5	460	385	285	115	75	5 + 5	2840
6	60 + 132	24 + 168	222 + 30	90 + 36	30 + 18	12 + 6 + 6	1560
7	126	21 + 105	49 + 42	35 + 49	7 + 21	0	707
8+	16 + 68	28 + 52	35 + 96		79 + 18	17	838
				131 + 88	25		
	1992	1772	1346	756	341	98	20744
	636	520	366	155	66	25	

TABLE V
BREAKDOWN FOR PURPOSE OF FURTHER INTERPOLATION

1953–4

£	0–1.0	1.0–1.5	1.5–2.0	2.0–2.5	2.5–3.0	3.0–3.5	3.5–4.0	4.0–4.5	4.5–5.0	5.0–5.5	5.5–6.0	6.0–6.5	6.5–7.0	7.0–8.5	8.5–10.0	10+
persons	822	1500	3889	5000	6088	5080	4000	3366	2700	2100	1513	1100	734	1300	924	964

1969

£	0–2.0	2.0–2.25	2.25–2.50	2.50–2.75	2.75–3.00	3.0–3.25	3.25–3.50	3.50–3.75	3.75–4.00	4.0–4.25	4.25–4.50	4.50–4.75	4.75–5.00	5.0–5.25	5.25–5.50	5.50–5.75	5.75–6.00
persons	89	61	78	92	110	133	163	203	257	297	323	348	378	404	427	461	480

TABLE VI
PER CAPITA DIRECT TAXATION (THE RAW FIGURES)
1953

Household original income range	< £156	156–312	312–415	416–519
1 person households:				
a Original income	21	174	353	453
b Direct benefits	109.2	59.5	25.4	21.3
c Direct taxes	1.2	14.1	48.2	62.1
d c/(a + b) as %	0.9	6.0	13.0	13.1
e (a + b) per head	130	234	378	474
2 adult households:				
a	60	159	345	456
b	92.4	155.7	56.6	48.5
c	6.9	5.6	29.8	45.7
d	4.5	1.8	7.4	9.1
e	76	157	201	252
2 adults, 1 child:				
a	89	202	377	475
b	32.4	122.1	65.4	60.3
c	0.7	14.8	25.1	32.6
d	0.6	4.6	5.7	6.1
e	41	108	148	179
2 adults, 2 children:				
a	82[a]	–	364	458
b	266.6	–	111.3	116.4
c	7.2	–	25.2	25.7
d	2.1	–	5.3	4.5
e	87	–	119	144
2 adults, 3 children:				
a	74[a]	294[a]	–	440
b	345.6	215.3	–	165.0
c	5.6	20.5	–	26.2
d	1.3	4.0	–	4.3
e	84	102	–	121
2 adults, 4 children:				
a	117[a]	182[a]	385[a]	–
b	352.6	381.9	274.2	–
c	8.7	13.2	25.5	–
d	1.9	2.3	3.9	–
e	85	94	110	–

[a] Printed in wrong column in source?

1953

520–727	728–1039	1040–1559	1560–2599	2600+
579	792	1346	2064	3033
19.0	19.7	11.3	11.3	11.4
96.0	160.2	352.6	606.6	1163.7
16.0	19.7	26.0	29.2	38.2
598	812	1357	2075	3044
616	849	1210	1910	4273
39.2	30.6	29.3	29.6	41.3
69.5	113.6	222.5	374.5	1880.7
10.6	12.9	18.0	19.3	42.7
328	440	620	970	2157
624	834	1227	1904	4043
63.0	69.9	70.1	62.0	73.6
52.1	89.0	207.4	450.1	1693.2
7.6	9.6	16.0	22.9	41.1
229	301	432	655	1372
602	823	1204	1909	3192
122.9	126.0	124.5	124.8	149.7
36.0	67.6	173.1	426.2	1132.1
5.0	7.1	13.0	21.0	33.9
181	235	332	508	835
578	798	1245	1847	3318
174.7	188.4	173.8	191.0	174.8
27.8	51.0	162.6	431.8	1201.7
3.7	5.2	11.5	21.2	34.4
151	197	284	408	699
545	746	1095	1722	3686
257.2	274.6	270.0	205.2	225.7
26.9	36.9	97.8	302.5	1398.5
3.4	3.6	7.2	15.7	35.8
134	170	228	321	652

Table VI (continued)

1969

Household income range	< £260	260–314	315–381	382–459
1 person households:				
a Original income	63	291	347	421
b Direct benefits	375	263	241	216
c Direct taxes	2	21	25	44
d c/(a + b) as %	0.5	3.9	4.2	6.9
e (a + b) per head	438	554	588	637
2 adult households:				
a	82	289	347	418
b	588	480	506	518
c	0	21	17	36
d	0	2.7	2.0	3.8
e	335	385	427	468
2 adults, 1 child:				
a	–	–	–	–
b	–	–	–	–
c	–	–	–	–
d	–	–	–	–
e	–	–	–	–
2 adults, 2 children:				
a	76	–	–	–
b	800	–	–	–
c	11 [b]	–	–	–
d	1.2	–	–	–
e	219	–	–	–
2 adults, 3 children:	–	–	–	–
a	–	–	–	–
b	–	–	–	–
c	–	–	–	–
d	–	–	–	–
e	–	–	–	–
2 adults, 4 children:				
a	–	–	–	–
b	–	–	–	–
c	–	–	–	–
d	–	–	–	–
e	–	–	–	–

[b] Income-tax is negative, doubtless due to refunds. I count, therefore, only national insurance.

1969					
460–558	559–675	676–815	816–987	988–1195	1196–1447
513	620	737	899	1093	1310
231	163	98	74	102	106
64	90	112	149	245	284
8.6	11.5	13.4	15.3	20.5	20.0
744	783	835	973	1195	1416
509	618	750	904	1090	1313
472	431	326	218	206	148
32	67	98	146	176	222
3.3	6.4	9.1	13.0	13.6	15.2
491	525	538	561	648	731
–	612	771	909	1097	1324
–	413	277	278	191	190
–	40	78	92	139	178
–	3.9	7.4	7.7	10.8	11.8
–	342	349	396	429	505
–	629	753	908	1087	1329
–	594	412	382	304	306
–	16 [c]	43 [b]	76	94	171
–	1.5	3.7	5.9	6.8	10.4
–	308	281	304	324	388
–	–				
–	–	767	914	1096	1332
–	–	469	534	486	495
–	–	38 [b]	105	100	164
–	–	3.1	7.3	6.7	9.0
–	–	247	288	316	365
–	–	–	888	1108	1308
–	–	–	758	657	663
–	–	–	42	121	143
–	–	–	2.5	6.9	7.3
–	–	–	274	293	329

[c] Income-tax is 3. I have counted it as zero, since it is between two negatives.

Table VI (continued)

Household original income range	1969 1448–1751	1752–2121
1 person households:		
a	1577	1918
b	79	88
c	395	515
d	23.8	25.7
e	1656	2006
2 adult households:		
a	1604	1926
b	119	91
c	292	354
d	17.0	17.6
e	862	1009
2 adults, 1 child:		
a	1587	1913
b	170	180
c	239	293
d	13.6	14.0
e	586	698
2 adults, 2 children:		
a	1606	1929
b	300	282
c	212	308
d	11.1	13.9
e	426	476
2 adults, 3 children:		
a	1587	1913
b	467	529
c	206	284
d	10.0	11.6
e	411	488
2 adults, 4 children:		
a	1614	1938
b	688	632
c	168	293
d	7.3	11.4
3	384	428

1969		
2122–2565	2566–3103	3104+
2345	2854	–
59	45	–
534	729	–
22.2	25.1	–
2404	2899	–
2315	2817	4726
99	90	77
439	576	1300
18.2	19.8	37.0
1207	1454	2402
2315	2801	4050
196	170	120
400	440	759
15.9	14.8	18.2
837	990	1390
2323	2779	4450
284	311	320
409	457	911
15.7	14.7	19.1
549	658	965
2328	2849	4358
467	480	435
361	439	797
12.9	13.2	16.6
559	666	959
2290	–	–
674	–	–
282	–	–
9.5	–	–
494	–	–

TABLE VII
PER CAPITA DIRECT TAXATION (CONSOLIDATED) IN PERCENTAGES OF INCOME

Gross per capita income from all sources	1 person	2 adults	2 adults 1 child	2, 2	2, 3	2, 4	Inferred weighted average [b]
			1953 [a]				
74 (= P5)	n.a.	1	1	1	1	1	1
90 (= P10)	n.a.	2	2	2	3	2	2
125 (= P25)	1	3	5	4	4	3	3
171 (= median)	4	7	6	5	4	3	5
245 (= P75)	7	9	8	7	9	8	8
333 (= P80)	11	11	11	13	15	16	11.5
429 (= P85)	13	13	16	17	22	25	15
			1969 [c]				
200 (= P5)	n.a.	n.a.	n.a.	0	n.a.	n.a.	0
240 (= P10)	n.a.	n.a.	n.a.	1	3	2	1
335 (= P25)	n.a.	0	4	7	7	7	4
471 (= median)	1	4	11	14	11	10	10
702 (= P75)	8	15	14	15	13	n.a.	14
961 (= P80)	15	17	15	19	17	n.a.	16
1185 (= P85)	20	18	17	n.a.	n.a.	n.a.	18

[a] Includes employers' as well as employees' contributions to national insurance.
[b] The weight is of course the numbers of people in the per capita income bracket.
[c] Excludes employers' contributions. But so does original income, so net incomes are the same.

taxes we must turn to other sources[3], which have had access to the full FES data. See table VI.

We obtain the corrections for income tax and national insurance shown in table VII. Note that Mr. Nicholson does not cover every kind of family. Children are overrepresented in our data. I have interpolated and smoothed, but not at all violently.

6. I conclude that income inequality very slightly increased in the U.K. in 1953–69. This seems to be the conclusion of most workers in the field: I here name those workers whose methods are arithmetical rather than intuitive or merely ejaculatory.[4] These results and other similar workings, yield the comparable per capita income distribution of table VIII, all gross of income-tax (except figures in parentheses).

[3] For 1953, J.L Nicholson in *Income and Wealth*, Series X (1965), pp. 147, 152. For 1969, *Economic Trends,* February 1971, table 2(i). The FES data on income tax in 1953 are much too low, and I use here Nicholson's corrections. The 1953 income tax is the most doubtful part of this whole analysis.

[4] Paolo Roberti of the Centre for Studies in Social Policy (7 Arundel St., London W.C. 2), privately circulated, Sept. 1973. Covers 1949–67. Deciles V–IX have gained from deciles I and X. This study is based on the Central Statistical Office series that was terminated in 1967 because its compilers had no confidence in it. The units in the upper deciles are income-tax units. Those in the lower deciles are probably "nominal income-tax units"!

Stark 1972. Also income-tax based, but reduces the tax units to per capita incomes. Concludes no change or slight increase in inequality 1949–63.

Nicholson 1967. Same as Roberti.

The stock of wealth, however, has become much more equal. Here are A.B. Atkinson's best estimates (1972, p.21 for 1911–13; privately circulated for 1960 and 1969): [footnote continues on p. 49]

TABLE VIII
OUR GRAND RESULTS (per capita income)

	U.K	U.K.	U.S.A.[a,e]	Italy[g]	Hungary[a,h,i]	Poland[a,c,i]	Czecho-slovakia[d,e,i]	Bulgaria[f,i]	U.S.S.R.[b,e,i]
	1953–4	1969	1968	1969	1967	1967	1965	1963–5	1966
semi-decile ratio	5.7(5.0)	5.9(5.0)	13.3(12.7)	11.2	c.4.2(c.4.0)	n.a.	4.5(4.3)	3.84	6.0(5.7)
decile ratio	3.6(3.3)	3.9(3.4)	7.0(6.7)	5.9	3.0(3.0)	c.3.1	3.2(3.1)	2.73	3.7(3.5)
quartile ratio	1.9(1.8)	2.1(1.9)	2.6	2.5	1.8	1.8	1.8	1.65	2.0
P50/P5	2.3	2.35	4.2	3.4	2.0	n.a.		2.1	n.a.
P95/P50	2.5	2.5	3.2	3.3	2.1	n.a.		1.8	n.a.

[a] Wiles and Markowski, 1971 (corrected).

[b] From table III in Lecture I. Socialist sector only.

[c] Covering only 80% of the population, but including the extremes.

[d] Statistička Ročenka 1967, pp. 461–3.

[e] Deducting 5% arbitrarily to allow for the income tax on the top decile and semi-decile. For the probable actual impact of the U.S. and Polish income taxes cf. Wiles and Markowski 1971, pp. 361, 364.

[f] Statisticheski Godishnik 1971, p. 407. Workings available on request.

[g] From data supplied by the Banca d'Italia. Omits auto-consumption, owner-occupiers' rents, interest and dividends. Consists mainly of employment and social service incomes net of such income tax as is deducted at source. Workings available on request.

[h] Hungary has the smallest of all Communist income taxes. I have deducted 5% from the top semi-decile alone, to allow for its impact on private incomes. The reforms were in 1968. They certainly redistributed income: from workers and bureaucrats to managers and peasants. This might well not affect our ratios.

[i] Omits owner-occupiers' rents.

My ratios of skewness are the proportions of the median to each semidecile. P50/P5 shows the success obtained in abolishing poverty and P95/P50 that in reducing great wealth. My international comparison (U.S.A. – U.K. – Italy) differs greatly from other workings. This seems to be due to:

insufficient comparability of definition in other workings;
the subtraction of the British income-tax here;
my foolhardly advance outwards to the semi-decile;
the use of mere averages, such as Gini's, by others;
my insistence on per capita, not per family, income;
bad data, both here and elsewhere.

7. In a field where the data are so bad, other indicators than income must be sought. I can think of only one other reasonably inclusive indicator of welfare that is as good. Indeed it is statistically much more reliable, and could replace income altogether, could it only be shown to be a reliable proxy. This is age at death. The rates by social class have moved as shown in table IX, where the *Standard Mortality Rate* is the ratio of the observed number of deaths in a given social class to the expected number of deaths, i.e. the number of deaths one

Percentage of total private wealth in the U.K.

In the hands of	Top 0.5%	Next 0.5%	Next 4%	Centiles 95–91	Centiles 90–1
1911–13	69		18	5	8
1960	28.2	8.8	25.6	12.0	25.4
1969	21.6	8.4	24.2	15.1	31.7
1973	23		24	16	37

1973 is by Alan Day in the Observer, 3 Feb. 1974. These figures exclude all pension rights and are weak on the household goods of the poor. They therefore understate the movement towards equality.

TABLE XI

al	Weights in population (%)			Standard mortality Rates ages 20–64			Infant mortality per 1,000				
	'31	'51	'61	'31	'51	'61	'31	'49	'51	'65	'61[a]
ied women											
	2.7	4	4	81	96[b]	77	33	24	19	13	15
	16.2	16	16	89	88[b]	83	45	27	22	16	18
	48.5	52	50	99	101	103	58	33	29	19	22
	16.8	15	19	103	104	105	67	34	34	20	24
	15.7	12	7	113	110	141	77	41	41	24	29
	bottom 26% ÷ top 20%[a]			1.24	1.19[b]	1.40	1.68	–	1.75	–	1.42
e women											
	0.4	1	1	100	82[b]	83					
	8.6	17	13	(64)	73[b]	88					
	57.4	41	43	95	89	90					
	8.1	19	18	102	89	108					
	3.1	5	2	112	92	121					
-	22.3	18	23		(142)	(115)					
ːd											
	2.5	3	4	90	86[b]	76					
	14	16	15	94	92[b]	81					
	49	52	52	97	101	100					
	18	16	20	102	104	103					
	16.5	13	9	111	118	143					
	bottom 29% ÷ top 20%[a]			1.14	1.21[b]	1.44					

[a] Interpolated by me.

[b] The method used by the Registrar General is to set the number of deaths registered betwee
·9–53 and 1959–63 against the Census Population of 1951 and 1961 respectively. For 1951
possibly for 1961 as well, there is a marked discrepancy between the occupational de
ption given in the Census schedules and in the death registers, the overall effect being to
ggerate the mortality rate in Social Class I and underestimate that in Social Class V. A cor
ion was made, and is shown, for males only.

rces: Registrar General Decennial Supplement; 1931, 1951 and 1961; J.A. Heady and others
cial and Biological Factors in Infant Mortality", The Lancet, 1955; C.S.O. Studies i
lical and Population Subjects, No. 19. My workings available on request.

would expect in the social class if the average death-rate for England and Wales was applied to it. It is a measure of the divergence of any given social class from the average. We introduce, then, in this table, the notion of the *distribution of mortality* among quantiles of the population. We are less interested in the Registrar-General's social classes than in the underlying income distribution. His low-numbered classes are indeed richer than his high-numbered ones, though alas not for each individual. So we can only approach, not attain, the ideal of a distribution of mortality by per capita income.

The absolute mortality rates of class V, after the age of 35, even increased slightly between 1951 and 1961. We can only speculate on the reasons for this surprising development:

(i) The definition of class V has changed to give higher weight to accident-prone occupations. But this is not true of the bottom 29% of men, and it does not explain the similar fate of married women. However, it seems reasonable to argue that the occupations of the top 71% have become relatively and absolutely less dangerous. This view is partly confirmed by the tables on death rates from specific causes by social class. In 1961 there was a positive gradient for "other accidents" as well as for "accidents in the home" and motor accidents. These gradients were all negative in 1951 (by positive gradient is meant that the S.M.R. increases from class I to class V).

(ii) More of class V survived the dangerous first year. This incontestable improvement makes it very probable that more survived for 20 years; but there was perhaps not sufficient gain in real income to keep its members alive until retirement. I am inclined to put much the main weight on this explanation.

(iii) Instead of an improved pattern of consumption, there *may* have been an increase in conspicuous consumption, motorbikes, consumer durables and so on, and in "vice" consumption, tobacco, alcohol, at the expense of an improved diet. The tables on the causes of death by social class seem to confirm this view. For example, between 1951 and 1961 there has been a switch from a negative to a positive gradient in coronary and lung diseases as well as in deaths from hypertension, and, as noted above, "consumption accidents." Simultaneously the rich were beginning, under pressure of medical propaganda, to abandon over-eating and smoking.

(iv) The poor have failed to make, or to be allotted, as much use of the National Health Service as the rich.

(v) Finally a point hard to interpret: the new classification of occupations introduced in 1960 is different in some important respects from previous classification.[5] The main difference is that each individual is assigned to his proper social class, as determined by his occupation. If he is of management status, he is then upgraded by one social class. This is an important change; possibly in previous years the tendency was to lump anybody of management status into class I, which must have raised its S.M.R. Also the armed forces were excluded from the social classes in 1961, while they had been included in previous years.

All in all, our death rates more or less, but only more or less, confirm our income figures. Death shows itself to be a poor proxy for income, since it depends very much on a few narrow consumption categories, notably medicine and food. It is thought, for instance, that despite very gross inequalities of income upper-class Romans did not much outlive the poor, because they used lead plumbing, which the poor could not afford. Only some of the causes of death are synonymous with income.

[5] See Registrar-General op.cit. 1961, p. 18.

LECTURE III

REGIONAL INEQUALITY

1. The result, that the U.S.S.R. is less equal than the U.K., is surprising. It does not command confidence. Perhaps, however, it is statistically right but morally misleading: the U.S.S.R. may have greater historical and geographical inequalities to overcome. So we turn to the regional question. The U.S.S.R. is a very big country, so surely it is bound to show more inequality on that ground alone? Surely the amount of social and fiscal effort required to keep a country equal rises as its size increases? There are at least two a priori arguments for this point of view.

The first is a rather trivial matter, affecting, say, the first centile only. The larger the country, quite apart from regional variations, the larger tend to be those organizations that can be large: ministries, political parties, churches, trade unions, corporations. Therefore the heavier the responsibilities of their leaders. But the larger the country the greater also the absolute number of highly intelligent and capable people; so both demand and supply rise. However, supply rises only in proportion to the number of people, while demand rises more rapidly than that, since wholly new types of sophisticated senior responsible post are created, while the number of old-fashioned senior responsible posts keeps pace with the number of people. Simultaneously the absolute yield of taxes rises, so that the people at the summit of political power, who are not much more numerous, can take more per head. The Emperor Akbar was incomparably richer than Queen Elizabeth I, though his subjects were poorer.

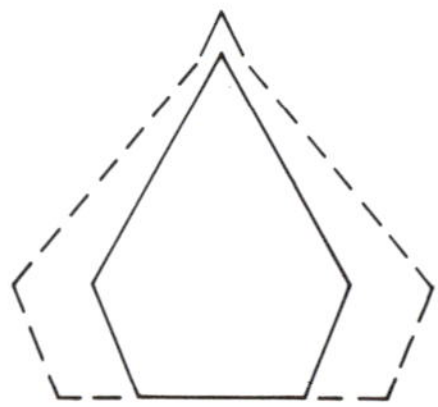

Fig. 1. ——— = small country. – – – – = big country.

Thus ceteris paribus the pyramids of earned incomes expand in proportion to the population except at the very top, as in fig. 1, where ceteris paribus refers to the level of development, the socio-economic system in force, etc. It is evident that this argument is not watertight and should be checked factually. But it does give the U.S.S.R. a plausible excuse for inequality at, say, the top centile. However, we know little about any top centile, and at the semi-decile no such excuse can be urged.

2. The second a priori argument affects far wider circles of people: big countries have regions with deep historical differences. Yugoslavia is almost alone among small countries in this: no big country is without it.[1] Now could the presence of

[1] Indeed large geographical extent may impose historical regional inequalities on quite small populations: Canada, Brazil. The only exception to this sub-rule may be Australia.

regional differences *not* affect national indices of family inequality? I.e. suppose we are egalitarians, must we not soften our moral judgement on the U.S.S.R. in view of its greater objective difficulties? Or to put it another way, is it not a group of egalitarian regions, the averages of which history has separated, while the U.K. is a group of inegalitarian regions whose history has not been so divisive? We have no distributions of family income for named regions, the average income of which we know, in either country. We shall only be able to use a priori reasoning.

At the extreme, with each family defined as a region, there is no difference between the two kinds of inequality. For more complicated cases I can present no complete mathematical theory. It seems, however, that a mathematician could endlessly use his ingenuity to think up special cases in which the existence of regions with unequal *averages* did not raise, or even lowered, this or that total inequality *index*. But they are all utterly unreal. If regions have more or less lognormal curves like nations, and the means or medians of these curves differ, the nation will be more unequal than it would have been without such regions. This is the overwhelmingly probable case.

For simplicity we have only two regions:

———————— poorer region P,
– – – – – – – richer region R,
· · · · · · · · · · · total nation T.

The vertical axis is numbers of people, the horizontal axis is log wealth. I_p, I_r and I_t are any acceptable index of inequality for the regions and the nation. We suppose first that all distributions are uni-modal, and that $I_r = I_p$.

We examine first the gap between two such regions. In fig. 2a the regions are little dispersed, and the lower national decile contains *abc* people from P and *yzc* people from R. In fig. 2b P is further impoverished, and the points *a*, *b* are displaced by the same log distance as the median *d*. The national

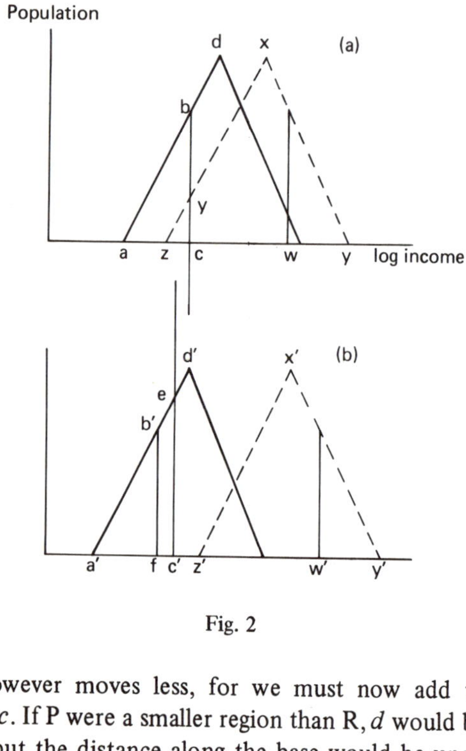

Fig. 2

decile however moves less, for we must now add the area $b'ec'f = yzc$. If P were a smaller region than R, *d* would be lower than *x*, but the distance along the base would be unchanged. Then *bc* would be short, and therefore *cy* would be long, and the lower decile would move little if at all. But then by parity of reasoning the upper decile would move further.

Until the overlaps are cleared the increase in *dx* always exceeds the increase in *cw* where *w* is the top decile. If there are no overlaps the increase is the same. Already in fig. 2b there is no overlap at the semi-decile, so if that had greater weight in our index, inequality would go up more. Clearly *the more extreme indicators of individual income are more sensitive to regional dispersal.*

3. Now in the U.K. and in the U.S.S.R. without kolkhozniki the distance *cw* is about the same; but *dx* is greater in the U.S.S.R. with kolkhozniki than in the U.K. (see below). Putting the same total population and the same scale of income, we prove greater family equality in each Soviet region thus. First we simply assume that the Soviet *dx* without kolkhozniki would be smaller, but still not so small as in the U.K. There can be no doubt that regional differences are particularly marked in the traditional peasant sector, so our assumption is very hazardous. Anyhow, to achieve the Soviet effect we put the U.K. as fig. 2a, and the distance $d'x'$ in fig. 2b as an indicator of Soviet regional dispersal. How could $c'w'$ be restored to the length *cw*? Clearly only by elongating the triangles, or raising d' and x', so that they are higher than d and x. Therefore each Soviet region is more equal than each British region. And this is what we set out to prove.

It is beyond my mathematical powers to exceed two regions. But I do not think the assumption of two regions was misleading. Thus suppose there are many regions, all equally egalitarian, and the relations only of the averages of the middle ones change. Then even the national decile ratio, let alone more extreme ratios, will not be much affected. If the extreme regional averages change, all the ratios, even including such an uninteresting one as the quartile, are affected, for the extreme regions are of course heavily represented in the middle of the nation. But the extreme national ratios will be more affected. If we take a very large number of regions – at the extreme again defining each family as a region – even if intra-regional equality is absolute there can be very great nation-wide inequality, depending now wholly on inter-regional dispersal.

None of this seems to alter our conclusions based on two regions. Therefore the U.S.S.R. is indeed partly excused her high national inequality index by her size, provided that her observed regional inequalities mostly arise in the socialist sector. Only if we knew a great deal more could we say how much excuse she had. Table II gives such regional averages as we know.

4. Now let us turn aside from regions sensu stricto to consider the kolkhozniki as a group. If we could include them would they make the nation-wide inter-family distribution more or less equal? Any social class or race (say Jews, gypsies, South-East Asian Chinese) forms a "region". The kolkhozniki were a poor "region" of about 21.6% of the total population in 1970. They enjoyed 16.0% of the income[2], and they also exhibit great internal inequality between both families and regions, for which we have no data. 55 years after the revolution, neither their poverty nor their inter-family inequality is historically excusable. It is tempting to suppose that in this case $I_r < I_p$.[3] So we are considering a two-"region" society in

[2] Deduced from Sarkisyan 1972, pp. 167–72. However, we must repeat the warning that the imputed rents of owner-occupancy are not counted in Soviet statistics. All kolkhozniki, but only 1/3 of the rest of the population, are owner-occupants.

[3] But this is not so in Hungary (*Statistical Yearbook*, 1968, p. 326). Working peasants are only very slightly more unequal than gainfully occupied workers and employees. The same seems, on a superficial examination, to be true of Bulgaria (*Statisticheski Godishnik* 1971, p. 407), and of the individual peasantry in Poland (Wiles and Markowski 1971, p. 490). It is of interest that U.S. negroes – one of capitalism's

which the regions are of differing inequalities. Our specific question is whether the omission of kolkhozniki leads us to under-estimate or over-estimate I_t in the U.S.S.R.

The matter is very simple. If one region (or class, or race) blocks out a disproportionate part of one tail of the national distribution (since its mean differs from the average mean),

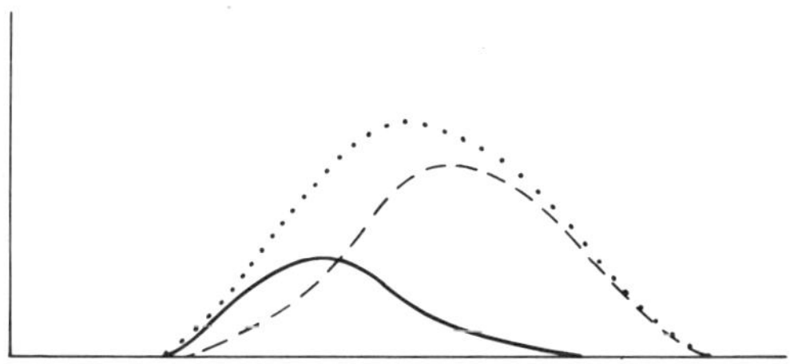

Fig. 3. The case of the Soviet co-operative (poor) and socialist (rich) sectors. The total is at each point the sum of the other two.

then the other region, or the sum of the remaining regions, is more equal than the nation. And this holds whether the first region is more or less equal than the nation. This is illustrated in fig. 3.

The value of I_p was not made particularly distinct in fig. 3. Let us now do so in two extreme versions (figs. 4 and 5). It clearly makes no difference to the basic proposition that $I_r < I_t$.

Only if we relax the assumption of continuous and unimodal regions can we think of cases where both I_p and $I_r > I_t$. The perfect case is fig. 6. But cases of bimodal regions or nations can also be imagined that do not produce these results,

near approaches to the kolkhozniki – have a less equal distribution than the national average.

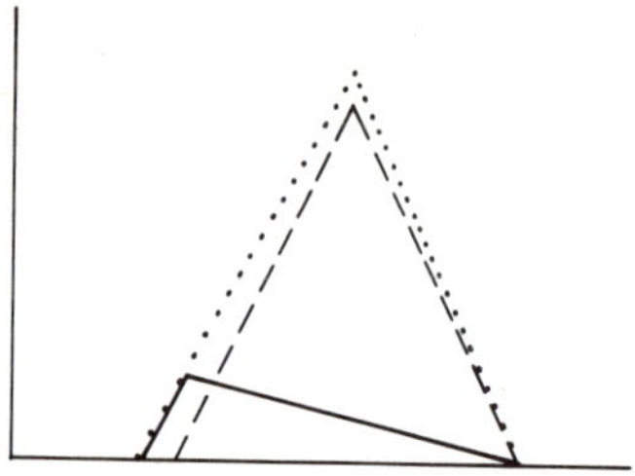

Fig. 4. Extreme cases of fig. 3: in 4 $I_p > I_t$, in 5 $I_p < I_t$. But I_r always < I_t.

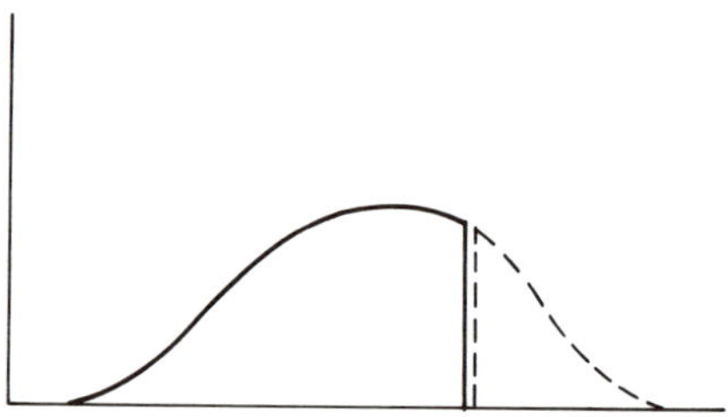

Fig. 5. Rich and poor parts of a town divided by the proverbial "railroad track".

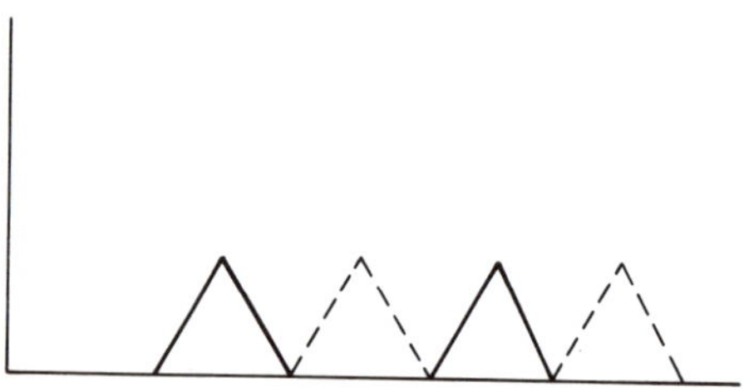

Fig. 6. Two bimodal regions. $I_t < I_p = I_r$.

and in any case empirical experience produces very few bimodal and no discontinuous distributions. Most of these are for small samples, with the modes close together. Bimodality is therefore a chimera (let alone discontinuity) and we must simply accept that the total Soviet distribution is less equal than the non-kolkhoz distribution.

5. Suppose there had been more than two of these "regions". How would changes in intra-regional inequality have affected national indices of family inequality? It is clear that such changes in the middle "regions" would have had minimal effect: moving a few percent of the total population this side or that of the quartiles. If we are right at all in concentrating on the extremes, movements within the extreme regions are more important, since they have far more effect on the decile and semi-decile ratios. But this concentration becomes now itself questionable. If rich Slovenes become richer and poor Slovenes poorer, how much does this matter to a poor Kossovar? For it is with him, and not the poor Slovene, that we compare the rich Slovene when we look at the Yugoslav semi-decile ratio.

I incline to say that in highly regionalized countries we must eschew national indices of inequality. For it is exactly true that they make us compare rich Slovenes with poor Kossovars, but the point of such an exercise is not obvious. In the case of classes or races, however, the national index of inequality is the whole point. It is entirely fair and right (though not possible) to construct a Soviet index including kolkhozniki, even if it were preferable to have several regional ones.

6. So much for the kolkhozniki. We now turn to the data on actual regions, which are too little known. Note that in all

countries we have to content ourselves with politically, not economically, defined regions. Usually this is quite satisfactory, since the differences are of long historical origin, and economics and politics coincide.

A more troublesome question is the regional price index. Our figures concern only consumer prices, so surely somewhat understate the variations. For building prices vary tremendously, and much affect the interregional comparison of investment. In particular a cold climate raises both building and consumer prices, especially the former, and most large countries have climatic differences.

Over and above this, we should not even be comparing the same basket of goods in a cold and a warm climate; for the former we need more heat, clothing and food, i.e. a larger basket to compare the cost of "living" at the same level of human welfare, whatever the prices are. This is perhaps not the place to enter too deeply into this question. There appear to be no data on it whatsoever, except the Soviet ones quoted below. But just as a foretaste of its complexities, note that there is an important distinction here between rich and poor countries. To the poor the heat of the sun is an almost unalloyed benefit, allowing them to dispense with the housing, food and clothing that the cold imposes even on them. But the rich demand air conditioning, which is very expensive. And all these comparisons were neglected by our inter-family distributions, which were no more deflated for inter-regional than for interclass differences in the cost of living.

The evolution of the Soviet republics is now available, owing to the work of native researchers and the care of Wagener (1972) and Wilber (1969). The latter covers the early period, for which we have no regional figures for national income, and presents an index for the growth of 14 basic products and services in Central Asia (including Kazakhstan) and in the

TABLE I
CENTRAL ASIA VS. U.S.S.R., 1928–62

	Wilber's index of absolute performance, corrected		Annual growth rates (%)		
	1926–8	1960–2	The index unadjusted	The index adjusted	National income per head, adjusted
Central Asia	149.8	994.9	6.0	6.0	
U.S.S.R.	341.0	1502.8	4.5	6.0 [a]	4.9 [a,b] or 6.9 [a,c]

[a] Subtracting 8 years for the war.
[b] Ruble factor cost of 1937.
[c] "Composite, 1937 base". Cf. Wilber p. 5 and Bergson 1961, p. 217.

U.S.S.R. as a whole. The total index is the unweighted sum of the international index numbers for Central Asia and the U.S.S.R. with respect to each product in 1928 and in 1961. These latter indices are of the form Qc/Qf or Qu/Qf, where c = Central Asia, u = U.S.S.R. as a whole, and f is France in 1960–2.[4] We obtain, with France = 1400, the indices shown in table I.

It is obvious that the index, putting the U.S.S.R. above France, is bad at international comparisons. But it "predicts" Soviet national income growth accurately enough, because its 14 items are very basic and easily numerable, i.e. just the things that Communists concentrate on. It is also not very far out in "predicting" interregional differences, as the next table

[4] Details, including my arbitrary corrections to Mr. Wilber's data and his own unpublished workings on the U.S.S.R. as a whole, available on request.

shows. I infer that Central Asia has caught up with the rest of the U.S.S.R. *only* because of the war-time destruction in the East, and the permanent evacuation of plant and labour to within its borders. In peace-time, non-recovery years growth has been the same.

7. For the "post-heroic" period of Soviet regional statistics, here are Wagener's figures (table II), based on domestic calculations of regional income.[5]

This table also presents guesstimates of the regional fluctuations in the purchasing power of the ruble. Our figures present a regional index of the cost of minimal subsistence for a single worker, making allowance for the climatic variations in the number of calories he needs, as well as price differences in the state and kolkhoz markets. Our sources are writing as experts who know what people should consume, and they do not compare what they actually do consume; their aim is a scientific basis for wage differentiation. But *faute de mieux* their data are very welcome. Indeed they are superior to mere interregional price indices, since they do make some allowance for the extra cost of keeping alive in a cold climate.

The original data are given in table III.

[5] Wagener 1973 also contains fairly good estimates going back to 1950, and very bad ones going back to 1940.

TABLE II
SOVIET REGIONAL INEQUALITY, 1958–68
(NET MATERIAL PRODUCT AT MARKET PRICES PER HEAD, U.S.S.R. = 100)

	Actual prices		1968		Population 1968
	1958	1968	Cost of living (very approx.)	Deflated income	
U.S.S.R.	100	100	–	–	231.8
R.S.F.S.R.	109	113	?107 [c]	108	127.9
Ukraine	100	98	100 [a]	100	46.4
Belorussia	68	82	?101.5 [g]	83	8.8
Moldavia	80	82	?100 [e]	84	3.5
Lithuania	93	115	?103 [d]	114	3.1
Latvia	129	144	?103 [d]	145.5	2.3
Estonia	119	141	?103 [d]	142.5	1.3
Georgia	77	65	? 92 [f]	71	4.7
Azerbaidzhan	83	61	? 92 [f]	67	4.9
Armenia	74	74	? 92 [f]	82	2.3
Uzbekistan	69	56	c. 95.5 [b,a]	59	11.2
Kirghizia	67	62	c. 95.5 [b,a]	66	2.8
Tadzhikistan	56	50	c. 95.5 [b,a]	53	2.7
Turkmenistan	83	57	c. 95.5 [b,a]	61	2.0
Kazakhstan	78	70	103.0 [a]	69.5	12.7
Top two ÷ bottom two =	2.02	2.69		? 2.53	

[a] Straight from source: see table III.
[b] Assuming no intra-regional variation in source's figure.
[c] See text below.
[d] Put by me at = rest of R.S.F.S.R.
[e] Put by me at = Ukraine.
[f] Must be lower than Central Asia since there is more smuggling and the climate is better.
[g] Put by me half-way between Ukraine and rest of R.S.F.S.R.

TABLE III

U.S.S.R.: STANDARD BUDGET FOR A SINGLE WORKER EXCLUDING DIRECT TAXES

	1968 [f]	c. 1966 [e]
Central	100.0 [a]	100.0
Urals	113.1 [b]	103.4
West Siberia	105.6 [d]	
East Siberia	118.2 [c]	107.7
Far East	127.1	116.6
Ukraine	97.6	87.1
Central Asia	93.2	83.2
Kazakhstan	100.5	101.2
Far North of Yakutia and Magadan		158.4
Oblasti to South of these		132.8

[a] Excluding Moscow city, including Moscow oblast', Smolensk, Yaroslav.

[b] Sverdlovsk and Chelyabinsk oblasti.

[c] Irkutsk oblast', Krasnoyarski krai.

[d] Therefore means such places as Novosibirsk, Barnaul, Omsk?

[e] Sarkisyan and Kuznetsova 1967, p. 85.

[f] Kapustin and Kuznetsova 1972, p. 52.

Thus the omitted areas are: R.S.F.S.R. – N.W., Volga, North Caucasus, Volga – Vyatka, Central-Chernozem, Moscow city; Transcaucasia, Baltic States, Belorussia, Moldavia. It is as usual better to guess than to resign. So we convert the known areas of R.S.F.S.R. to Ukraine = 100 and add: Moscow city = 110, rest 103. Then, weighting by the population (in millions), we arrive at:

Moscow city	110 /6.6	East Siberia	121.2/ 7.3
Rest of Central	102.5/20.2	Far East	130.2/ 5.7
Urals	116.0/15.3	Rest of R.S.F.S.R.	103.0/ 60.7
W. Siberia	108.1/12.2	R.S.F.S.R.	107.0/127.9

The omitted smaller republics are guessed as shown in table II.

8. We see that regional equality has sensibly diminished, even before the recent threats of further diminution.[6] The phenomenon is evidently most intractable. Canadian, Yugoslav and Italian figures also reach back over time, and show no improvement over the U.S.S.R. Only the U.S.A., of the countries known to me, has been successful at equalization.[7]

We need also some instrument of international comparison. True to my suspicion of all mere averages like the Gini coefficient or the variance[8], and to my preoccupation with the extremes of any distribution, I choose the regional decile average ratio (RDAR). This is the ratio between the average of the regions in the top decile and the same at the bottom. It is thus not a true decile ratio, for that is between incomes at specific points, not averages.

I derive the Soviet RDAR as follows. Of the top 10% (23.2 mn.) 6.6 mn. lived in the Baltic States. The next 16.5 mn. must have lived in the Ukraine or the R.S.F.S.R.; put them at 105% of the R.S.F.S.R. average. This is not unfair, since 10 mn. of them lived in Moscow or Leningrad. This puts the top 10% at 117.5% of the Ukrainian average. The bottom 10% received, without guesswork, 61% of this average.

By this measure the U.S.S.R. is neither the worst nor the best of countries. Taking the other data from other workings, we arrive at the following RDARs:

[6] For one of these see President Podgorni in *Kommunist*, 8/1972. Questions of regional development will be decided "on a new basis": while the needs of individual republics will be taken into account, a great deal of investment will now be directed "where it is most needed from the point of view of the interests of the Soviet economy".

[7] Cf. Wiles 1974.

[8] Wiles and Markowski, 1971; Lecture I above.

U.S.S.R.	1968	1.93	U.K.	1961	? 1.53
U.S.A.	1969	1.38[b]	Canada	1971	? 1.75[b]
Yugoslavia	1971	3.53[a,b]	Italy	1970	? 2.8 [a,b]

[a] Not deflated for interregional price differences. [b] Wiles 1974

9. However, the U.K. also has a historical excuse for inequality quite inapplicable to the U.S.S.R.: immigration. There were about 1.7 mn. immigrants from poorer countries in the U.K. in 1971[9], whereas in the U.S.S.R. the equivalent figure was about zero. Unlike those to Western Europe, the immigrants to the U.K. have brought their families, and can vote: they are in no sense *Gastarbeiter*, indeed there are hardly any such people. This important distinction is not always appreciated. It is incidentally also important that immigrants have or develop nuclear families rather bigger than those of the natives, but of course they bring fewer old people with them. The whole movement has now ceased.

Now if the immigrant population has a distribution of skills and money capital like that of the natives, incomes may fall (say because of diminishing returns to natural resources) or rise (say because of economies of scale); but the distribution will only change slightly. The main effect of immigration on distribution will be that there are different elasticities of demand for various skills. I have no idea which elasticities are lower, but presume that these differences are random between low and high wages.

[9] 0.7 mn. Irish, 0.5 mn. Caribbean and African, 0.5 mn. from the Indian sub-continent. There was very substantial migration in and out by Anglo-Saxons, but the net figure was low. There were about 1.2 mn. other foreign-born, mainly Polish or from the white Commonwealth. Source: Census 1971, Advance Analysis, London, H.M.S.O., 1972, p. 103. I have counted the British-born children of these immigrants as natives.

But if the immigrants are mainly unskilled and without capital, inequality will increase even if they are all employed. Low wages will be lowered, and the numbers receiving them raised. This is of course very obvious in the short run, but in the long run there is a simple corrective mechanism: the expanded size of the economy creates more medium- and high-level jobs, since technology adapts itself only imperfectly to the changed skill structure. So much is clearly true, but we must now make a wild assumption: there is unexploited talent among both immigrants and natives, so that these jobs come to be filled after a time without trouble. I.e. the skill structure adapts itself to the technology and the old structure of wages recovers from the shock of the immigration: though other forces continue of course to act upon it, and notably technical change itself.

Much depends on how many years constitute a long run. If, as in the U.K., the immigration lasts 20 years, after 60 years almost no-one is an immigrant, for the first generation adults are dead and the second generation of children is mostly not foreign-born. But low skills are inherited, and the effect of the immigration might well remain. On the other hand, we would expect the labour force to start up-grading itself, and so restoring the skill pyramid to normal, at once. But the immigrants and their children would surely take a very long time to accumulate capital.

One way and another it is extremely difficult to set up a quantitative measure of the inequality caused by recent immigration rather than by the general features of the social system. But it is undoubtedly there. Suppose that of the 1.7 mn. surviving immigrants 0.7 mn. had fitted at random, on account of skill and capital, into the native population straight away; but that the other 1.0 mn. had all gone in below the lowest quartile, and that by 1969 the skill-upgrading process had had a negligible corrective effect on their impact. Then what was the effect on inequality? Our figures for 1969 (Lecture II, table IV) include the effect of immigration, so we proceed to reconstitute a population without it by subtracting these 1.0 mn. people (1.8% of the total) from the bottom quartile as given. We do so by taking 4 × 1.8% away from each group in this quartile, and recalculating all the inequality ratios. The semi-decile ratio falls by 0.25%, the others are not affected[10]!

Recent immigration, then, would not appear to be so good a historical excuse for inequality as regional poverty of long standing. From the excuses offered in this section the U.S.S.R. stands to gain more than the U.K. But we do not know any intra-regional distributions in the U.K.; and our Soviet ones (Lecture I, table III) are in fact almost as unequal as the national distribution.

[10] Workings available on request. It must be borne in mind that the top semi-decile is also shifted by the reduction of the total population.

LECTURE IV

ON THE REDUCTION OF TOP SALARIES

"A Gentleman always has as much money as he wants"
(Old English proverb)

"L'inégalité des talents doit aboutir non a l'inégalité
des rétributions mais à l'inégalité des devoirs" (Louis Blanc)

1. Of late two left wing distributive doctrines have gained much currency: that there should be equality of results as well as of opportunity, and that schools should neither discover nor encourage excellence.[1] With the second doctrine I am wholly out of sympathy. I hold all types of excellence to be extremely scarce and very useful to humanity as a whole. I think that children who have it often do not know it, and that though not as lazy and shortsighted as other children they are after all children; and what they lose early in life they may not catch up. I am entirely persuaded by the geneticists who tell us that under normal conditions of environmental variety the environment accounts for one quarter and the genes for three quarters

[1] Bell, 1972; Illich, 1971.

of the difference in intelligence between one person and another. So excellence cannot be manufactured, it must be discovered and promoted.

Since people are genetically unequal, and great abilities are too rare to be wasted, the distribution of power and prestige must be unequal. In these respects "equality of results", to refer back to the first doctrine, is incompatible with even moderate efficiency and not likely to be tolerated by ordinary people who, free of ideological blinkers, prefer to be doctored, ruled, managed, entertained and even lectured to by competent people. So far we are in entire conformity with Rawls' principles (Lecture V, section 1).

But need the preferential promotion of the excellent imply unequal wealth? Certainly the excellent, having been normal children, grow up into normal adults: they are greedy. It is not to them that we must look for an answer to this question, but to the government – in so far as it can be distinguished from them, and that is the main trouble. I believe that much greater equality of economic results than we at present see in the U.S.S.R. or the U.K. is compatible with economic efficiency. Moreover we must in a sense reverse the inequality of economic opportunity in order to make it so. Clearly equality of results is only possible where the able suffer a handicap.

My main point is that this is not inefficient, and does not necessarily mean paying the able less than their marginal product. For if *per impossibile* we were to reduce all top private salaries, fees etc. "at a stroke", everyone would continue to work as before, since there would be no competition to lure him away, and *the supply curve of any individual's total labour is negatively sloped*. This fact of negativity I take to be something too well known to have to be proved. I only draw the obvious, if much neglected, consequence of it here.

This elementary proposition is regularly misunderstood,

even by very well trained economists (Dean 1966, pp. 1–10, 81–2). If anyone denies it, he thinks, *by definition*, that leisure is an inferior good! He has probably fallen into one of the following traps:

(i) only primitive peoples have negative supply curves. On the contrary, nearly everyone has.

(ii) negativity is disproved if primitive peasants produce more of their cash crop when its price rises. On the contrary they have probably cut some unrecorded subsistence activity.

(iii) negativity is disproved if primitive peasants go to mine in South Africa (or British doctors to practice in USA) for higher incomes. On the contrary they increase their income by switching their jobs, partly *in order to* have more leisure.

(iv) negativity is irrational. On the contrary it is probably irrational to cut one's leisure as income rises. Precisely because it is now smart to believe that primitive peasants are economically rational, it is more attractive than ever to believe in negativity.

(v) the fact (if fact it be) that people work harder after economic development has taken place shows that the supply curve is positive. But development violates the normal *ceteris paribus* clause of any demand or supply curve; that it shows the reaction of a person of unchanged tastes to changes in a certain price alone. Just because this is stated in chapter 1 of every elementary textbook, we are not free to forget it. Besides, development in the West has obviously increased leisure.

Of course leisure could be or seem to be an inferior good: (a) it might become complementary to expensive leisure goods; (b) sheer opportunities for work might expand while incomes rose, and much leisure, if technically imposed on us in the opening situation, is very boring; (c) on promotion we often face the indivisibility of much more money and a little less leisure or no promotion. The argument here is subject to none of these qualifications.

Keynes strongly implied this very doctrine, of negative or vertical supply curves of total labour and of other services by individuals, in his celebrated passage on the excessive price of enterprise (1936, p. 374): "... it is not necessary for the stimulation of these activities and the satisfaction of these proclivities that the game should be played for such high stakes as at present. Much lower stakes will serve the purpose equally well as soon as the players are accustomed to them."

All I am saying is that this is true of salaries and skilled labour as well as enterprise – indeed top salaries do form part of the stakes of enterprise; and that the adequate functioning of East European professionals demonstrates the point. It is not that they do not want more, or are contented; they function.

2. What happens when the rich are systematically paid more than their opportunity cost? How could we show whether or not this was so? If (i) it was so only in a few enterprises and occupations the short lists for vacant senior posts would be longer or more distinguished than for "similar" posts elsewhere. The selectors would have a more difficult task, an *embarras de richesses,* but their difficulty would be a pleasant one, and soon over. Nothing else would be visible. Indeed in such a very imperfect market as is that for senior people it is hard to judge the similarity of posts or the distinction of candidates; so perhaps nothing would be visible at all.

If (ii) the higher salary levels for senior posts applied to all employers and occupations, no-one already in this market would be paid more than his opportunity cost any more! The discrepancy would only exist at the boundaries between senior and other posts. Those who entered directly the "executive" (business) or "administrative" (civil service) grades from university would receive noticeably more than other school leavers – or perhaps they would only be promised a high chance of later receiving noticeably more. Those who moved up into such posts later in life would suddenly get much more. Of these two classes only the latter would really notice anything. But selection committees would again have an *embarras de richesses* at these boundaries.

Thus, it would be very hard indeed to tell whether all senior posts, or even some senior posts, were being overpaid or not. But it would be easy enough to know if they were being underpaid: there would be few applicants, and selection committees would complain that quality was not what it used to be when they were young. There would be a state of disequilibrium, and corrective measures would be taken. *But none would need to be taken in the case of overpayment,* unless bankruptcy threatened. For to lower salaries just below one's own is to threaten one's own. It is even better, if the decision-maker is mobile and has no great stake in the equity, to accept one's employer's bankruptcy and take a similar salaried post somewhere else. Overpayment of people just below one has indeed no marginal productivity for the enterprise, but it surely has a high personal one to those who, a few rungs up the ladder, decide the salaries of their juniors and so their own.

It is evident from the first lecture that Stalin made some such mistake as this. There was a fortiori no automatic corrective tendency in a Soviet-type economy. Stalin paid higher differentials than were necessary, so he must have got longer short lists, or better short lists, for every senior post. This did not interfere with his system any more than the fact that English judges received £12,000 p.a. in 1812 – there just are only so many judgeships. So long as the poor do not revolt, we can always offer the rich more than is necessary: by increasing the competitive offer of competent people for each job we do not reduce the supply of competent people as a whole.

But the fact that Khrushchev could lower the inequality of salaries to U.K. levels without obvious trouble indicates, and the fact that Eastern Europe has perceptibly more equality than the U.K. comes close to proving, that we too can go further without obvious trouble. The increasing supply of graduates in U.S.S.R. cannot account for such sharp movements, or for their timing; or for the contrast with Eastern Europe. No doubt there is a lower limit below which people simply will not accept responsibility and the long hours that go with it: in other words, a point at which the opportunity cost of a manager is not some other managerial salary but a worker's wage.[2] But there is no reason to believe that we have reached that point, and it is our business to find it. I speak of course as a professor, who does not have to bear much responsibility. Undoubtedly I would have accepted the title and the prestige that go with it, and borne the minuscule extra responsibility and power, for no extra salary. But this explains only why I have been the one to develop such a theory; it does not disprove it.

3. A high minimum wage is different, and genuinely causes unemployment, because the act of hiring is performed by the same high-salaried people. In their own case they are almost distributing among themselves a bonus, but in the case of unskilled workers they adhere rigidly to their enterprise's demand curve. The right-wing complaint against minimum wage laws is correct: they discriminate against the cripple, the illiterate, the nomad, the invalid, the pensioner and other kinds of unlucky people, condemning them to unemployment and so raising the wages of their closest substitutes, the lowest-grade

[2] The kibbutz is an exception, but within kibbutzim there is direction of labour, particularly into managerial posts.

members of trade unions. Minimum wages only help the poor if, as in the U.S.S.R., enterprises are set legally compulsory targets for the employment of the unproductive. But this does not prevent capitalism from having instituted, by accident and without intention, an unrealistically high "minimum top salary".

This can, indeed must, be put in Illyrian terms: the managerial revolution and the divorce of ownership from control effectively constitute the management as a small Illyrian group of self-managers, with hired labour below them, but deciding on the general level of their own salaries with reference to profit available, not marginal productivity. They treat equity capital as hired capital – that is the definition of the managerial revolution[3]; and they distribute the "discretionary" funds available rather among each other. They have regard, of course, to a career structure, and to salaries offered by other enterprises. But these latter are similarly decided.

4. Illyrian behaviour would not be possible were not top managers a *non-competing group*. We must revive this useful theory, and abandon the pretence that the market, as opposed to chance, history or State edict, governs the pay relations between such groups. Labour and capital do not compete except at a few insignificant margins. These margins matter for those at them, but not for the bulk of labour and capital. Within the two great sectors imperfections of competition deprive the inter-sectoral margin of influence. The two-sector elasticity of substitution, beloved of high growth theory, is an ex post figment of the theoretical imagination. It is derived

[3] Their legal power to do so may well rest on their holdings of equity capital. These are valuable to them not for dividends but for power, especially the power to set their own salaries and fringe benefits.

from what has happened between two categories so broad as to be meaningless. It does not describe the ex ante processes of entrepreneurial decision on new techniques. Within the factor labour, young and unskilled people compete, and so do people with similar skills. But senior, responsible people have a rare non-competing skill. They are a closed group. Their pay relative to each other's is determined by the market; their average absolute pay by emigration, chance, or themselves.

5. Thus the macro-problem has a quite different solution from any particular micro-problem taken in isolation, but your[4] terms of reference prevent you from considering it. Therefore you will always come up with wrong solutions to the micro-problems with which you deal. Broadly, the existence of some differential at each point is rational, but its absolute size, and therefore the total spread of incomes from top to bottom, is a matter of custom and initial chance, reinforcing itself by competition within the bounds thus established. Marginal productivity is a truthful and fruitful theory of wages and hiring which I actively support, but no man's, above all no top man's, marginal productivity is accurately known, so the doctrine can justify a whole range of salary offers. Moreover each salary tends to be a percentage of the one below, and so "competitively" determined by it. But these percentages are themselves arbitrary or customary, and lower

[4] "You" is the Top (public) Salaries Review Body of the British Government, and most of this lecture is the revised summary of the evidence I gave to them (now published with their permission) on 11 May 1972. I understand a "top salary" to be over £6,750 gross in May 1972. There seems to be very little relevant economic literature, other than generalities on wages and salaries as a whole. Cf. however National Board for prices and Incomes, report no. 107, Cmnd 3970; idem, no. 132 Cmnd 4187 (includes bibliography); Wootton 1955; Routh 1965.

or higher ones could be used. But those who offer salaries also get them! Whereas those who offer wages get salaries. And those who write about salaries get salaries.

Suppose for instance that a rock-bottom, genuinely competitive salary for a young executive is £3,000 after tax. It is firmly believed that suitable men will *emigrate* (domestic competition can be controlled) if offered less here and now. They discount the prospects of promotion for both probability and futurity, so that the grade structure above them is a small but not negligible matter. Over this age and seniority emigration is not on, and there are five superior grades below the very top. History has placed these at 10% up over the one below. So the fifth grade is £4832. But the steps might as well have been 8 or 12%, and with our egalitarian bias we shall choose 8. Then the fifth grade is £4410. Already before the "very top", we have saved 9%. We may further assume that the salaried men who set salary scales have been over-generous at the bottom: the "oldest young executive liable to emigrate" can in all probability be retained for £2900, not £3000.

It is of course in the direct personal interest of the scale setters to make these errors, since it is their upward cumulation that determines their own salaries. Furthermore these are the lower rungs on the ladder they have themselves climbed, so that sentiment and professional solidarity strongly influence them. But more than that: we have to reckon with *social* solidarity. These young people are, not indeed often their own children, but the children of "people like us"; or at least they are socially assimilable – via the approved salary scale. It is remarkable in Appendix II that in the two countries where upper-class social solidarity is notoriously weakest the relative height of top salaries is lowest. Thus in U.S.A. nepotism, inheritance and snobbery are frowned on. It is supposed to be each man for himself: "if he'll come for less, buy him – he can look after himself, can't he?" And the Czechoslovakia of Novotny was the only Communist country to be governed by genuine proletarians with a genuine feeling that Communists ought to favour directly the manual worker.

It is history, i.e. war and inflation, that governs the relations between non-competing groups. Orthodox micro-theory has little to say, and large shifts take place that it cannot explain. A once-for-all shift has already happened three times in the U.K.: in 1914–8, in 1939–45 and from 1969 to the present day. The evidence for this is in Appendix II. Although some of it only concerns factor-shares, which are but dimly related to family shares (for which there are no pre-war data), the message is plain: the rich lost ground and the country survived. But there is also good evidence for a shrinkage of the salary scale in each profession. Such shifts also happened in all Communist countries at the moment of takeover, in the U.S.S.R. again (after Stalin's back-sliding) in 1956–60, and one seems now to be happening in Sweden and probably more widely. That it is to say, the thing can certainly be done, or can happen.

6. But should it be done? There are the following reasons for such a reduction:

(i) Some degree of equality is good as such.

(ii) High salaries are a rent of natural ability or of family advantage. Few people with high salaries have come up from the bottom, few have earned every penny.[5] So if in some sense

[5] Those unfamiliar with the figures tend to exaggerate social mobility. Cf. ed. David Glass, *Social Mobility in Britain*, London 1954. For an international comparison cf. Miller in *Current Sociology* (UNESCO) vol. 9, no. 1. Westergaard and Little provide figures for educational opportunity in *Social Objectives in Educational Planning*, OECD 1967. Cf. R.K. Kelsall et al., *Graduates, the Sociology of an Elite*, London 1972.

the money corresponds to marginal productivity, it still does not reflect individual merit.

(iii) We all feel the social system is unjust. This reduces our loyalty to it in crises such as war or inflation. Nobody *loves* a system in which "you get what you grab". For if marginal productivity reigns, subject to trade unions, within non-competing groups, the latter do indeed simply "get what they grab". This lack of love makes for *inefficiency* and *instability*.

(iv) Ministers, judges and employers (public or private) have to resist the wage-claims of people far poorer than themselves. This is their bounden public duty, lest the currency collapse. But how can they, when their salaries are so high? Remember Frank Chapple![6]

(v) Resentment of high salaries, and more generalized feeling as in (iii), play *some* part in generating union wage claims as well as weakening the resistance to them (iv).

Of course on a national scale the release of resources by a top-salary reduction would be inconsiderable. Moreover in connexion with (iii) and (iv) I have considered the (much more) unequal distribution of capital as outside my purview. But is is likely that resentment of that is a less powerful stimulus to wage claims. For the capital is distributed by inheritance and chance, which though blatantly unjust have at least "no damned merit about them". But a high salary implies a deliberate social valuation in relation to a low wage.

No one will do less work, quite the contrary. For, to repeat, the supply curve of each man's labour with respect to his

[6] Who, on behalf of the electricians' union, so acutely embarrassed the highly paid court of enquiry into electricians' wages and the highly paid government witnesses against his union's claim by quoting the witnesses' salaries and recent raises (cf. *The Times*, 19 Jan. 1971). Unfortunately Mr. Chapple himself accepted a large increase in salary not long after from his union.

whole income slopes backwards. This is a very simple little paragraph. Its substance is in its first two sentences. Yet it is of central importance for my whole thesis, and these extra words serve only to underline what does not need to be said at greater length.

The only solid justifications for paying anybody anything are (A) that you have recruitment difficulties for the job, and consider the job essential for your business. This is the pure marginal productivity doctrine, and it is undoubtedly true in a general way, though as we have seen it is hopelessly imprecise. To-day before my proposed general reduction, many salaries are above this justifiable minimum: e.g. mine (£5,876).[7] (B) The argument from personal efficiency is only that the man hired should be comfortable, healthy and free from care. This implies a level of £4,000 net at most: a sum without any a priori relation to the amount implied by (A). (C) There is also an argument from efficiency in relation to his work, to which we come.

7. The trouble with (A) recruitment is that people *emigrate*. This is the most serious objection to lowering top salaries. I do not believe that our entry into Europe will make much difference, since (a) it speaks foreign languages, (b) we can go there now, but we do not. (c) its top salaries are not grossly out of line with ours (see the Appendix), and (d) its inhabitants do learn English and are likely to come here, in a reverse brain drain. But North America is a serious threat and would be a greater one if top salaries were lowered. However, (e) the U.S. crime rates frighten many, (f) the general "quality of life" there is indeed lower, and (g) Canada, to which these

[7] In the money of 1971! Subsequently its real value shrank again, despite yet another nominal increase. History, then, is on my side.

strictures do not apply, is a small country with chronically high unemployment and waves of competing U.S. refugees!

The emigration argument makes me very uneasy, and I can only counter it with *contingent* facts about the likely countries of emigration. These facts, however, are very substantial, and they do in fact render it unlikely that lower top salaries would cause a brain drain. There is at present scarcely any long-run net brain drain. Junior doctors are an exception, however: a doctor's qualification is extremely "fungible", and the career structure in this country remains such as to create discontent among the ambitious. The other serious top salary cases are airline pilots and business executives in multinational corporations. Then come nurses, but they do not earn top salaries.

The point is so important that an emigration policy must be flatly recognized as an essential part of a top salaries policy. If, say, strikes and inflation continue here at their present rate and the Vietnamese War ceases, the argument from the "quality of life" will count against us. In many underdeveloped countries the possibility of emigration has produced an extremely acute top salary problem, with the equivalent of £4,000 net being not four times but twenty times an unskilled wage. This leads to very great social tensions, crises of conscience among young people etc. It is not too much to call this phenomenon a major cause of Trotskyism, Maoism, free-lance urban guerrillas, etc. Yet many Indians, Africans and Latin Americans, differing from these extremists only by a hair's breadth in their politics, must be paid £4,000 net lest they emigrate to the U.K., let alone the U.S.A.! It is therefore appropriate that your body should also on these grounds go beyond its terms of reference, to discuss the medical career structure in this country, international treaties controlling the migration of doctors, student loans not to be "called" except in the case of emigration, etc., etc.

8. Turning now to justification (B), in one way we are not free from care: inflation erodes our prospective pensions. All pensions must be fully indexated. This means issuing indexated (as to capital *and* interest) government bonds to private pension schemes. It means the full inclusion on the university and doubtless other quasi-public schemes under the Pensions Increase Acts. The trade-off between pension security and present salary is very great. I think most would accept a 5% reduction in after-tax high salaries in return for an indexated pension.

In relation to our work ((C) above), we must of course dispose of the required tools and appurtenances. These, however, are costs of the business, including legitimate expense accounts. They should not be part of pay. But there is a quite different argument based on the necessities of our employment, namely "headroom": a man must have much more money than his subordinates if he is to exercise authority. I do not believe in "head-room" since it is contrary to my personal experience. Authority goes with formal position, recorded experience and acknowledged skill. Money does not add much to it. I willingly accept power and glory and status: the extra pay is unnecessary. I do not think I am abnormal. The relation of my pay to my subordinates', both before and after tax, has become much more equal in the last six years without my perceiving any loss of authority.

This is not at all the same question as the opportunity for, and tax on, outside earnings. We must distinguish between this and head-room within a regular promotion structure. When we say that the marginal rate of income-tax is too high, we mean or should mean that it is too high on outside work. We have, however, already mentioned one reason why a professor's experience should not be generalized: the burden of responsibility lies lightly upon him. If he says something silly in a lecture he can always correct it next time without the university losing £10,000. He simply does not live so tense a life as a manager.

My main conclusion is that we must see top salaries as indefeasibly part of the whole pay, trade union and cost inflation problem. This is not only because unions are nearly as jealous of top salaries as they are of each others' gains. It is also because all incomes policies are devised and enforced by top salary earners, and so lose much credit. My own preference would be to take powers to freeze wages and salaries by decree – we need that anyway, to stop trade union leap-frogging. We should then unfreeze low wages one year before high wages and low salaries, and these again one year before high salaries. We should partially recompense the losers with indexated pensions: a measure clearly biassed towards the rich. This is not, however, the place to develop the whole scheme: my present aim is only to show that there is a top salaries problem, and that this is how it fits in.

9. Other conclusions suggest themselves. First, if at any later time income tax can be reduced, this should be mainly at the bottom end. But it was reasonable to lower the top marginal rates, and they must stay that way. For marginal recompense for extra outside work poses quite different questions from the promotion scales hitherto discussed. There is a genuine case for such recompense, which many rich people use as a blind when discussing their indefensible promotion scales.

Secondly we need much more control over *all* gross salaries in order to be able further to reduce our ridiculous penalties on extra work. The Soviet income tax is so admirably low just because of this. Direct legal control over top private salaries and fringe benefits is not too high a cost, if we can use it to free ourselves from the present absurdities of the income tax, and so allow the rich to do extra work.

There is even after Stalin still a top salary problem under Communism. That of the director of the Leuna-Werke in the D.D.R. is said by his West German friends to be astronomical, and a closely guarded State secret. Mrs. Furtseva, at that time in the Soviet Politburo, and trying to quell an industrial disturbance among that very well paid body of men, the Donets miners, was once asked her salary: she told the truth and created more disturbance. But it is still evident from the Appendix that Britain has more of a top salary problem than most capitalist countries for which we have information, and far more than Poland (Czechoslovakia, on the other hand, was generally thought by Communists to have gone, until recent years, too far).

Since these data affect only the top centile, they are in no way incompatible with our earlier finding that Britain is a very equal country at the semi-decile of family income per head. What they are is another nail in the coffin of the Gini coefficient and all other averages.

LECTURE V

REVOLUTION, CONFISCATION, INCOME DISTRIBUTION AND DEVELOPMENT STRATEGY

1. The first basic idea of this lecture comes from Lauchlin Currie (1966):

(i) The object of economic development should be to improve the lot of the poor, without too much thought either for the rich *or the national average.* This idea has been taken up very strongly by the I.B.R.D.[1], and is now common currency. The next two basic ideas are even commoner, and of no definable parentage.

(ii) Egalitarianism can in fact only succeed through anti-capitalist revolution: you have to *confiscate* in order to make a really serious movement towards equality. Confiscation is a frequent event and a feasible policy, both domestically and internationally.[2]

But (iii) confiscation is usually attended by civil or international violence, and this has large initial economic costs. The

[1] Cf. McNamara 1973.

[2] But the literature on it is minimal. On domestic confiscation cf. Bronfenbrenner 1955, 1963. For international confiscation see below.

disorders of the revolution itself prevent work and destroy capital; the revolutionary governments always make gross errors of economic policy, indeed worse ones than their predecessors; significant numbers may be killed or driven out; the country's diplomatic and therefore commercial position will probably worsen.[3]

Proposition (i) is moral. It bears a very strong resemblance to Rawls' principle of justice (1972): no inequality is just unless it may be reasonably expected to benefit the poorest.[4] Rawls seems to have developed his Social Contract myth in order to avoid making inter-personal comparisons of utility: in their mythical situations each person would maximise his utility by adopting his principle. But if we adopted it from an existing situation we could not avoid harming those presently rich, and the principle would entail very many severe inter-personal comparisons. So it is much more left-wing than the two classical criteria of welfare economics[5]: no *change* unless it may be reasonably expected to benefit *everyone* in his present position, either (a) in posse – the gainers *could* compensate the losers – or (b) in fact – the gainers *will* compensate the losers.

But justice does not necessarily include compensation. We do not compensate the burglars we imprison, nor, mostly, the polluters whose smoke we suppress. When justice is done, some people are unequivocally worse off in most cases. Welfare economics, then, is not about justice, since it refuses to make inter-personal comparisons of utility. It tries only to go

[3] All this is very obvious. The actual phrase "costs of revolution" may have originated with Bukharin 1922.

[4] Strictly not the poorest, but everyone, at the moment of signing a Social Contract that sets up a new society. Everyone is supposed to be ignorant of the position he will occupy, and to dislike gambling. So he looks from the point of view of the poorest.

[5] Cf. for instance Little 1950, chapter 6.

as far as it can toward justice while respecting every vested interest. This restriction permits very little sheer redistribution: only that of incremental income – and even there we must hesitate if expectations have already been capitalized, or if the increment results from someone's effort. It will be readily seen that neo-classical welfare economics cannot digest confiscation, indeed can hardly come to grips with redistribution. But it should be as readily evident that the market, and the whole lore of optimal resource allocation, can survive confiscation very well. All we need is that it be a rare event, so that confidence builds up again between times.

2. Propositions (ii) and (iii) are or pretend to be factual. Though both primarily political they have quantitative results which profoundly concern the economist. Cline (1972) also gives development sequences that concentrate on the poor. But he assumes all large political events and their economic consequences away. His "events" are, for instance, changes in the marginal propensity to import, or in the economies of scale. He would no doubt agree with me that nothing very interesting emerges from this analysis. But it was surely worth doing, since negative results are also valuable. My own interest, on the contrary, is to quantify the economic consequences of great political events.

Proposition (ii), that equality does not come about except through violence, is a bold one. In one way it is fairly obvious: private capital is more unequally distributed than income or education, so the best attack on inequality is to abolish private capital. This has never in fact been done except by a Communist revolution, so that is what we ought to have.

The argument is almost, but not quite, compelling. Here are three large qualifications:

(a) In the strict sense of real property, movables, securities and cash, private capital is not mainly inherited, since the dissaving of the ill, the unemployed and the retired ensures that rather little capital remains in their hands to be bequeathed. Most capital is in the hands of those who bought it with their savings.[6] However, this part is itself very unequally distributed, since the rich save a higher proportion of income than the poor, and get a better return on it too. So most of the personally accumulated capital is in the hands of the old who have high incomes. No wonder, then, that it has in fact been equalized substantially (p. 47).

(b) Consumer capital is also confiscated at the revolution, but nothing in existing Communist law or practice prevents its accumulation *de novo*; there are not even any death duties. Peasant/artisan capital is subject to low maxima in Poland and Yugoslavia; elsewhere it is collectivized – but that is another, and a long and sad, story.

(c) Indirectly we all inherit our capacity to earn: education, intelligence, thriftiness, connections, even accent are all mainly inherited, quite apart from the straightforward nepotism practised in small capitalist enterprises. And in any settled society that preserves the nuclear family (including, of course, Communism) this kind of inheritance persists, as is shown by the unequal social origins of students at Communist universities.[7]

[6] Statistics are in their infancy here. It seems that in the U.K. and the U.S.A., if we include inheritance by widows of their husbands' life savings, 40–50% of private capital is inherited. We should deduct about 15% in order to exclude widows. Cf. my forthcoming *Economic Institutions Compared*, chapter 16.

[7] Cf. Zev Katz in *Problems of Communism*, May–June 1971; David Lane, *The End of Inequality? Stratification under State Socialism*, London 1971; Frank Parkin, *Class Inequality and Political Order: Social Stratification in Capitalist and Communist Societies*, London 1971; Seymour Lipset and Richard Dobson in *Survey*, Summer 1973.

Indeed earned incomes per recipient may occasionally be more unequal under Communism than their capitalism, as in the U.S.S.R. 1935–55 (see Lecture I). This is a far cry from a greater inequality of earned and unearned family incomes per head, but even that occurred during the period of high Stalinism. However, all this was but a temporary phase in the history of only one Communist country, and that phase is now over.

The history of Britain seemed until 1969 to confirm the necessity of violence. It is true that the landed aristocracy and the greatest millionaires have suffered since about 1900 – witness the fates of their stately homes. But nothing much had happened to those slightly less rich than that, except during the two world wars. As we see in Appendix II, the wartime measures achieved a pre-tax redistribution which has never since been undone. What the rich, or the factor capital, gave to the war was only partially restored to it by peace. The poor, or the factor labour, took the rest. The pre-condition for this quasi-revolution was the spirit of unity and self-sacrifice brought about by *external* violence.

Mere taxation has had, at least until 1969, little further effect. It has been so easy to evade that its main result has been Protean changes in the *forms* of the incomes of the rich, or in their *places* of origin or enjoyment: salary raises become stock options or new expense accounts, companies register in and people retire to small islands whose principal export is tax evasion, legacies are anticipated by gifts *inter vivos*, etc. etc. It is impossible that successive British governments, of allegedly varying political complexion, should have been for 20 years unaware of these loopholes, or have thought them to be in conformity with the spirit of the law. We must therefore infer a deep organisational and spiritual complicity among nearly all politicians with the present degree of tax evasion, especially, be it noted, taxes on capital. It is particularly noteworthy that successive Labour governments introduced no capital gains tax, despite the successful U.S. example. So it was not unfair, even if probably wrong, to suggest that only more violence (including the indirect effects of external violence) could bring about the fundamental changes, whatever they might be, that must precede a campaign against tax evasion.

It is true, however, that social services and income subsidies to the poor – which are not much[8] evaded! – really can be extracted from a rich population without violence, and really have taken the sting out of extreme poverty. Certainly Britain and other West European countries show that, and the U.S.A. is now following suit. The U.S.A. is a remarkable contrast to the stagnation of West European inequality indices, but then the U.S.A. has only recently developed a Welfare state.[9]

This apart, we note that it is not impracticable (Lecture IV), and may well be more effective, to control pre-tax incomes than to tax. Such control is clearly much more difficult in a market economy, where not only, as usual, the sellers but also buyers of labour are independent of the government. A Soviet-type economy, which controls the pre-tax distribution of income, has no need for redistributive taxation, and does not use it. So tax evasion, which is as elsewhere substantial, is not regressive.

3. As to our basic proposition (iii), there are very few smooth revolutions in fact. The curious truth is that revolutionaries never do learn. Guinea, Cuba and South Yemen have

[8] Nevertheless there is the take-up problem: many poor Britons are too proud or too little informed to collect their due under this or that rubric.

[9] For the West European stagnation cf. Zacchia 1974. My U.S. data stem from the Bureau of the Census. They show quite beyond a peradventure falling inequality of family incomes until 1970.

TABLE I[a]

Year and policy	(1) The bourgeoisie (3 families)	(2)	(3)	(4)	(5) The proletariat (60 families)	(6)	(7)	(8)	(9)	(10)
	Gross of income taxes & subsidies	(of which unearned)	Net total	Average individually disposable	Gross of income taxes & subsidies	Net total	Average individually disposable	Profits of state enterprises	Net National Income at factor cost[f] (1+5+8)	Terminal rate of growth of (9) (% p.a.)
I	35.0	(26.0)	30.0	10.0	64.0	66.0	1.10	1.0	100.0	
III A	36.4	(27.1	30.0	10.0	66.6	68.6	1.14	1.04	104.0	
V A	37.8	(28.2)	31.0	10.3	69.3	71.6	1.19	1.08	108.2	2
B	35.7	(26.5)	31.5	10.5	65.3	67.0	1.12	1.0	102.0	
V B	38.0	(28.1)	33.8	11.3	69.3	71.0	1.18	1.0	108.3	3
III C	37.8	(28.2)	30.8	10.3	69.4	73.4	1.23	1.0	108.2	
V C	40.2	(29.9)	32.6	10.9	73.6	77.8	1.30	1.06	114.9	3
III D	23.0	(15.0)	20.0 [c]	6.7	62.0	66.0	1.10	7.0[h]	92.0	
V D	10.0 [d]	(1.0)	8.0	2.7	68.0	72.0	1.17	20.0	98.0	
VII D	10.0 [e]	(1.0) b	10.4 [e]	3.5	72.0	77.0	1.28	24.0	106.0	4
III E	8.0	(1)	11.6 [c]	3.87	56.9	60.9	1.02	10.1	75.0	
V E	3.0	(0)	3.0	1.00	62.0	66.0	1.10	19.0	84.0	
VII E	3.2 [e]	(0) b	3.44 [e]	1.15	66.0	71.0	1.18	23.0	92.2	4

Footnotes on pages 94-95.

Table I (continued)

Year and policy	(11) Indirect taxes & Subsidies	(12) Net investment [g] (14+15+16)	(13) Consumption of all kinds at market prices (9+11–12)	(14) Net savings by bourgeoisie & corporations	(15) Net savings by proletariat	(16) Net savings by state	(17) State and collective consumption (13–3+14–6+15) [g,j]	(18) Real income of proletariat (index number) [k]
I	5.0	7.0	98.0	5.0	1.0	1.0	8.0	100
III A	5.2	8.4	100.8	4.9 [l]	1.04 [m]	2.5	8.14	104.0
V A	5.4	8.7	104.9	5.1 [l]	1.08 [m]	2.5	8.48	108.2
III B	5.0	7.3	99.7	5.6 [p]	1.0 [p]	0.7	7.8	101.1
V B	5.3	7.7	105.9	6.0 [m]	1.06 [m]	0.64	8.16	107.1
III C	5.0	6.9	106.3	5.0 [q]	1.0 [q]	0.9	8.1	110.5
V C	5.3	7.3	112.9	5.3 [n]	1.06 [m]	0.94	8.86	118.4
III D	8.0	4.0	96.0	–5.0 [r]	–1.0 [r]	10.0	10.0	97.8
V D	16.0	18.0	96.0	0	0.3	17.7	16.3	98.9
VII D	20.0	20.0	106.2	0.1 [s]	0.7	19.2	19.4	103.0
III E	8.5	0	83.5	–5.0 [r]	–1.0 [r]	6.0	10.0	88.6
V E	13.0	13.5	83.5	0	0.5	13.0	15.0	91.7
VII E	18.0	17.8	92.4	0.07 [s]	0.7	17.0	18.7	94.5

[a]Arabic numerals are in units of currency; Roman numerals denote years; capital letters denote growth strategies. A = "normal", B = "Chicago", C = "populist", D = "Polish", E = "Soviet".

[b]The remaining assets in (2), apart from those of the tolerated big farmers, have now been smoothly nationalized without further loss of efficiency. They operate at a lower profit rate, set administratively.

[c]Note that these figures are inflated by dissaving.

[d]The heavy income taxes on the rich are turned, via lower salaries or confiscation, into state profits.

[e]The rich are now fully integrated into the new society and begin to draw on its social services. They are only liable for the very low income-tax on socialist earnings.

[f]This represents also growth in real terms.

[g]Factor cost assumed identical to market prices. So these columns are also in real terms, like (9). Foreign capital transactions are also set at zero throughout.

[h]1 unit from year I plus 6 units due to the nationalization of part of col. (2). As efficiency falls and wages rise, the assets originally in (2) yield only 21 units in all.

[j](17) also = (11) + (1) – (3) + (5) – (6) + (8) – (16). This identity incorporates our assumption of budgetary balance.

[k]According to the following formula:

$$\frac{(6)_n/\pi + \frac{1}{2} \times (17)_n}{(6)_\mathrm{I} + \frac{1}{2} \times (17)_\mathrm{I}},$$

where π = the cost of living index, and corrects only for the rise in indirect taxes:

$$\frac{(13-17)_n}{(13-17)_\mathrm{I}} \times \frac{(13-17-11)_\mathrm{I}}{(13-17-11)_n}.$$

The first formula assumes that under A, B and C 45% of (17) is useless from the point of view of a consumer, and that 5% of it goes to the rich; while under D and E 50% of (17) is useless.

[l]Though they have as much income as before, the rich react favourably to the higher income tax. After year III their savings then grow with their net incomes again.

[m]Savings grow with net incomes.

[n]The rich have by now recovered confidence in the system, and S/Y rises nearly to the proportion of year I.

[p]The rich, encouraged by the sharp tax reduction, have a marginal propensity to save of 40%. The savings of the poor remain high since they face greater uncertainty through the social service cut.

[q]The poor do not save a great part of their large increase in income, since they come to rely on the social services. The rich save nothing more, since tax takes 43% of their marginal income.

[r]All private saving ceases, owing to fear and uncertainty. Later it picks up at a much reduced rate, in the state savings banks.

[s]Having previous habits of thrift, the erstwhile bourgeoisie save a higher percentage of their income.

had costs of revolution quite as high as China, and China had costs higher than Eastern Europe. Perhaps there is a real historical generalization here: only very crude, brave and economically ignorant people actually make revolutions, and they are always perforce the immediate post-revolutionary rulers. But crudity, ignorance and bravery are extremely poor economic counsellors, and initial disaster always follows, only yielding to success when, under a different sort of leader, things settle down.

4. So I present in table I several alternative development sequences that separate the rich, the poor and the average (or total), and take explicit account of the possibility of confiscation, the unlikelihood of non-violent redistribution, and the costs of revolution. I begin in year I with a "typical" underdeveloped country, of about the level of Currie's Colombia. The proportions are based upon an idealized Colombia, which differs from the real Colombia of 1968 mainly in having far smaller state savings[10], and so less investment. I.e. I imagine for year I a clinically pure country which has had no aid or advice. Its people coldly contemplate what is the quickest way to raise the welfare of the poor, and they look into the future along five socio-economic development sequences, two of which are revolutionary. These sequences are all *Idealtypen*. The numbers are very, but not wholly, arbitrary. Different arbitrary figures would have led to substantially different results, but these initial figures and parameters do not reflect

[10] I am indebted to my student Gilberto Gomez-Arango, S.J., for the actual figures for 1968, and for many bibliographical references and ideas. In the real Colombia the second semi-decile of the population takes 13% of the national income, and the lowest nine deciles 52%. I have amalgamated these.

unfairly the prospects of a lower-middle class country about to embark, or not to embark, on revolutionary development. Moreover, this is how people *ought* to think.

Though the sequences bear names, like "Soviet", they do not describe what actually did happen in, say, the U.S.S.R. For instance, the course of events in that country in 1917–38 was a good deal more catastrophic than the one here postulated, owing to a prolonged civil war, a famine and the forcible collectivization of agriculture. Again the "Polish" Idealtypus is more favourable than the reality in 1949–60, since the Korean war, with the frantic re-armament and crazy preference for heavy industry that it brought, is assumed away. The sequences, therefore, are short novels: they illustrate but do not demonstrate. All figures are numbers of units of stable currency, and the population is stable. The poor are assumed to have no unearned income, but are allowed to save small quantities. Income distribution between one rich man and another, or one poor man and another, is taken to be irrelevant: the country is simplified into two classes, and our interest is focussed on transfers between them. With equal unrealism, we assume budgetary balance and foreign trade balance throughout. Nevertheless not everything is arbitrary. Income must equal expenditure, sub-totals within one sequence must bear a reasonable relation not only to each other but also to sub-totals within another. It will be observed that the yield on capital (2+8) is 27 points, that on labour (1–2+5) 73 points. The two Communist sequences show shifts in paid-out factor-shares that result from administrative/fiscal decisions rather than from technical change.

5. Policy A is the *standard* Western prescription for a mixed economy. State saving is sharply increased (by 1.5% of the original national income: col. 16). This is financed partly by

the buoyancy of the revenue, but mostly by seriously enforcing the income tax (1–3). The yield rises by 36% in 5 years, and the disposable income of the rich is frozen for 2 years: compare IIIA with I. The social services paid out to individuals in money are frozen during this initial period, the poor receiving the same net income transfer (2.0) in year III as in year I. State consumption is also frozen (col. 17). Otherwise there is little organizational or social change. Attention is focussed on the national average, but after year III social services increase, so that the net transfer towards the poor is 2.3 by year V. The distribution of gross income, the social services, the incidence of taxes and the savings ratios do not change thereafter, and growth is at 2% per head per annum.

Policy B is the *"trickle-down"*: tough-minded non-welfare capitalism. The welfare of poor people is neglected in the short run in favour of growth. The rich are positively encouraged to make money, as this is what makes capitalism work. Specifically, net direct taxes on the rich are reduced. Indirect taxes are held down, there are no further acts of nationalization, and profits of state enterprises are frozen. Social services, both direct (6–5) and indirect (17), are reduced by as much as the government dares. State energies are concentrated on monopoly control, tariff reduction, etc. At first national saving and income do not rise so rapidly as under A, since monetary policy is more deflationary; but after year III the more profitable employment of labour and capital has its effect, and growth rate settles down at 3% per annum.

This terminal rate is set so high not because I personally believe that laissez-faire raises growth, but for illustrative purposes that will become clear. But the right-wing case is not completely without prima facie support: we may think of Pakistan, with its few very rich men and its neglect of East

Bengal[11], outpacing socialist, egalitarian India, or Kenya outpacing Zambia. Be that as it may, it is indisputable that in due course the new wealth will "trickle down" through the market demand for labour. Distribution between rich, poor and government, and between saving and consumption, remains fixed as in year V. We further posit that there is no trade cycle, because Chicago-type monetary policies are used successfully!

Policy C is Currie's, more or less; perhaps the name *populist* is the least misleading. It was the policy of Felipe Pazos in Cuba in 1959, after Castro took power but before he went Communist. A moderate and merciful government takes one more unit from the rich and gives two more to the poor. It has no great faith in advanced technology so it freezes investment, and also uses capital so as to maximize employment rather than income, which is yet another way of giving more emphasis to the income of the poor than to that of the nation. In the same radical, non-socialist spirit, it freezes indirect taxes and the profits of state enterprise. It finds itself forced by its improvidence to cut collective consumption and state savings. Growth, initially 4% while employment rises and capital-intensity falls, drops after year III to 3% when the low rate of investment and the highly redistributive taxation take their toll. It does not drop lower because of the adventurous monetary policy and the willingness to use exchange control. Note in all these cases how negligible the amount of redistribution is, by the time it comes to an end. Thus if we take (7)/(4) as our index of inequality, the poor start out with 11% of the per capita disposable income of the rich. Under policy C they end up with 12%, while under B they get 10.5%, under A, 11.5%. Yet the changes in government policy are very large, and such as to cause passionate electoral politics, not to say

[11] I leave this as it was written in 1970.

disorder. Thus under C transfers are doubled, while under B they are reduced by 15% and frozen for 5 years in the face of 8% growth. Over a period of 7 years, society is almost immobile except through revolution.

Policy D is "Polish": private tangible capital is confiscated, except from peasantry and artisans. The richest among them still draw the remaining 1 point in col. (2); the mixed income of the remainder is submerged at all times among the labour income of the proletariat in col. (5). A Soviet-type economy is established in the predominant socialist sector, but a proper use of human capital is grudgingly allowed: the former bourgeoisie are still permitted to collect the high salaries to which their scarce talents entitle them in the labour market. Thus the bourgeoisie is never really liquidated as individuals, but only as a class, and passes, through more or less tribulation, into the new technocracy.[12] It even eventually saves again at a higher rate than the proletariat (VIID/14) – in whatever forms are now socially permissible. This policy is both revolutionary and efficient. There is of course a little disorder and the national income loses 8 points by year III:

[12] All this has been true only of Poland among all East European countries. Yugoslavia, for instance, went through a very destructive phase before conforming to this model. Furthermore she has not got a central physical command system, but a socialist market. It is not clear how this has affected the subsequent long-term growth of her socialized sector. Hungary's left-extremist phase was still longer, and she too has recently introduced a socialist market, with unknown consequences. However, her ex-bourgeoisie has survived better than the Yugoslav, although her agriculture remains collectivized. The D.D.R. has preserved her ex-bourgeoisie very well (except from emigration). She collectivized her agriculture sooner than she nationalized her small industry. Czechoslovakia has been as tough as Hungary was to begin with, and continued like that. Romania and Bulgaria had but a small bourgeoisie, and were extremely severe with it. Otherwise they resemble Czechoslovakia.

capital (2+8) 5 points and labour (1–2+5) 3 points. After year V the 4% growth rate characteristic of Communism sets in. But investment funds are always used less efficiently, so that the savings proportion has to be greater than under B or even A for the same rate of growth. Indirect taxes rise sharply, as well as state profits. This makes possible a rise in wasteful state consumption (administration, police, propaganda) and in genuine collective consumption (education, health, public entertainment). This latter is distributed, as always under Communism, at random between the rich and the poor. The rise of indirect taxes raises the cost of living, so we must deflate to obtain the real growth of consumption.

Policy E is *"Soviet"*: all private capital is confiscated, agriculture is collectivized, crafts are suppressed (I have brought collectivization forward into the earliest years, for simplicity). The skills of the bourgeoisie, rich peasants and artisans are mostly wasted. Their earned incomes are reduced to those of the poor and – and this is more important – they are allocated almost at random on the labour market. The new technocracy arises at random out of the whole post-revolutionary population. The ensuing redistribution among the former poor is therefore not shown in our sequences, so the ultimate degree of inter-personal inequality is not less than under D, although our index of inequality does not show it. This policy is revolutionary and inefficient. Tremendous losses must be incurred before the Communist growth rate of 4% sets in. Investment funds are used as inefficiently as in D.

6. Col. (18) gives the deflated real per capita income of the poor as an index number; the formula is in the notes. While it takes account of collective consumption it does not take account of personal capital. It neglects the effect on the welfare of the rich of the Communist confiscations; and of the losses

or dissavings forced upon the poor by the chaos of the revolution. On the other hand, the poor do not need now to save so much, and this is also neglected.

7. We tend to the conclusion that if the *ultimate* material fate of the poor is our principal concern (column 18) the immediate politics of the government, even the choice between blue capitalism and red revolution, is neither here nor there. This is of course because we have in each case put a term to the period of redistribution; so that the growth of the income of the poor coincides in the end with that of the national income. The terminal rate of growth, then, is what matters.

A strong government is certainly able to destroy the luxuries of the rich, and bring about equality. Certainly, too, it can mobilize money for investment. Moreover, the "costs of revolution" can be placed on the shoulders of the rich alone: the poor need hardly suffer at all, as in case D. This is what most actual Communist revolutions did: though some, notably the Soviet one, blundered into making life intolerable for everybody. This simple point throws light on those cases where the revolutionaries drive out the rich, as in Algeria or Czechoslovakia in 1946 (the Sudetens, who were expelled before Czechoslovakia went Communist), or again in Cuba. Naturally the national average falls, but this tells us nothing about the income of the poor.

But if the politics or policy of a government can effect the ultimate rate of growth, then those who are solely concerned with the *ultimate* level of column (18) should prefer that government. We shall not, in a lecture already grossly too general and superficial, further pursue this well-worn path, except to point out that with the figures we have chosen "Poland" presents the best choice. It will be further observed that we have left out the unsuccessful Chinese and Cuban strategies altogether: for these two countries have added to the costs of revolution a low terminal rate of growth.

Concern for the poor is not the same as desire for equality, let alone justice. The attempt actually to implement, from an existing situation, what appears to be Rawls' principle might hurt the poor very greatly. For that principle is not, in existing situations, what it appears to be. It becomes quite conservative, though still remaining far from welfare economics. For there is a great gulf fixed between an actual revolution and a mythical social contract. The material interests of the poor could even have been, with only slightly different arbitrary figures, better served by B, the "trickle-down", than by any other policy.

We have twice emphasized the word "ultimate", because in the near future, and so also if we sum many years together, things are very different. Thus simply comparing catch-up times, the level of the poor under D at a given point in the time catches up with: A in 7 years, B in 12, C in 23. And E catches up with: A in 11, B in 12, C in 32 years, but it never catches D at all. However, we should compare growth paths, not growth points. Integrating the growth paths indicated by column (18) we find that B catches up A in respect of total consumption over time during the 10th year; that C is ahead of them at all times; and that D catches up A in the 19th and B in the 27th year. But it is only in the 43rd year that D catches C. E behaves much like D with a lag, catching up for instance A in the 26th year.

If we apply a rate of futurity discount D and E become quite untenable policies. But it is not obvious why we, as planners or moralists or Colombian politicians, should do this. If it is true that posterity has no provable claim upon me, it is no less true that I have no claim on it. The futurity discount is surely only an observation of how people do behave; it has no normative status. It plays, to be sure, a very conservative (so not necessarily right-wing) role in politics, because all change, including counterrevolution, creates initial disturbance; but it is not clear that it should be permitted to do so.

It is obvious that a smooth revolution with minimal take-over costs would indeed cause a great difference. It is equally obvious that nothing harms the poor so much as a failed revolution, for that gives us the costs without the benefits. A revolution is an investment and comports a risk. This risk like all others must be subjectively estimated but has an objective existence. It is not at all like the futurity discount with which it is normally amalgamated in action and thought. In a very general way I would put the odds against a revolutionary attempt, taken at random from human history, at three to one. This is a much more serious conservative argument than the futurity discount or the costs of a successful revolution.

8. We conclude with some grave qualifications and warnings. First, our omission of the balance of payments is particularly serious: not only is the balance certain to go into deficit during the troubles but having, or not having, a revolution might bring a country a great deal of foreign aid. Confiscation is itself a form of foreign aid, saving often several percentage points of the national income annually, which would have had to be paid in debt service. Indeed the best procedure at present may be first not to have the revolution, and so to collect aid from the one side, then to have it, repudiate the debt and collect aid from the other side. But particular small countries may find that unchanging loyalty to one or other system pays off better, in the diplomatic situation where they find themselves, i.e. revolution and confiscation have extremely important international aspects which I have neglected here (Wiles 1969, pp. 405–8; Haq 1973).

Indeed there are at least three types of semi-revolution, where violence is used and confiscation is partial, that often run smoothly and incur minimal costs. The first two we have met. One is the great equalization of pre-tax incomes in Britain during the last wars, and probably by most belligerent welfare states. This war was, for British domestic purposes, a semi-revolution. The second type is to repudiate foreign debt only, without internal violence. The third is to reform a "feudal" land tenure system, on which the urban capitalist and state bureaucratic classes do not feel their fate depends. It is not suggested that these actions run no danger of high costs, or are easy to carry through in circumstances of domestic tranquillity. I only point out such a happy conjuncture is wholly possible and has often happened. The risk of failure is less, and the cost is less; for of course the cost rises with the risk.

Lastly our choice of Colombia, a "lower middle class" country, was prejudicial. The magnitudes would be substantially different in a very backward, or in an advanced, country. Where we are already at subsistence level we cannot afford the costs of revolution, because we die: China and Indonesia have had much less happy economic histories since 1945 than India and Pakistan.

On the other hand, advanced capitalist countries have more equal income distributions than that shown. The analysis into only two classes of "rich" and "poor", a gross over-simplification anyhow, becomes here a travesty. *Some* governmental re-distribution of income becomes a reality, and especially tends to eliminate the all-important "very poor"; though at the top end its effect seems, on long historical experience, to be slow. Outside mere formal redistribution there are free public education and Keynesian full employment policies. Also rich countries probably respond differently to changes in development strategy: for instance laissez-faire becomes less attractive, since there are so many potential public entrepreneurs. Moreover, the "terminal" rate of growth is now far more dependent on new technical progress and accumulation alone. I.e. in middle-class countries systems are differently good at mobilizing resources, especially at importing old technical progress; but in rich countries systems make less difference. Again revolution and confiscation are now *seen* as in the interest only of the very poor, for whatever the facts about them may be, everybody else has something to lose and thinks he will lose it. Certainly everybody will be at risk, but it is still true that revolution and confiscation would bring about far greater equality.

APPENDIX I

OTHER SOVIET DATA

1. With so much interpolation and roundaboutness, every crumb of confirmation is necessary. First I adduce R. and R.'s figure on their page 168. They say that it shows how similar are the distributions of earnings in Poland and the U.S.S.R., but to my mind it shows how different they are! They say "in the same year" without naming it, and they use the unusual word *rabotniki* for "workers", which has no accepted statistical definition. However, virtually the same Soviet curve is given by Mozhina (1961), and it is there stated to be for manual workers (*rabochie*) in 1959 (see fig. 1). The numbers along the bottom axis are Mozhina's (her scale is 15 to R. and R.'s 7, whatever that may imply): she puts both modes at 1.0, a step I cannot explain, if the bottom axis is fractions of the median. It would further appear that the Polish median is to the left of the Soviet one.

Perhaps then only the general shapes of the curves are reliable. It is not contradictory that, using Loznevaya's data for 1966, Markowski and I (1971, p. 505) found the distribution of Polish and Soviet earnings per worker and employee to be about the same. For it is in the U.S.S.R. that there has been most equalization.

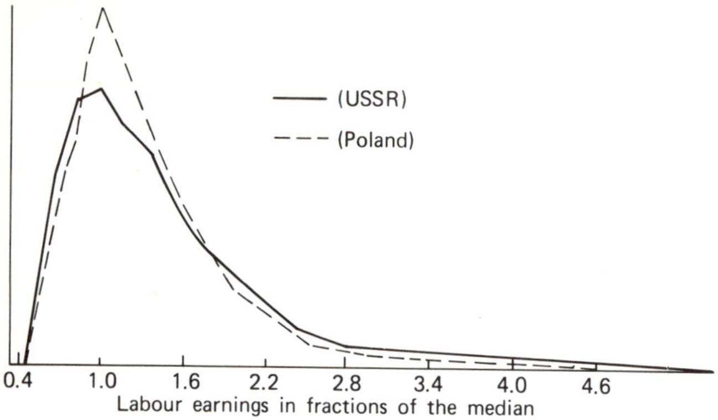

Fig. 1. The distribution of workers by the size of their labour incomes, 1959.

2. The second confirmatory evidence is from I.I. Korzhenevski's (1965 and 1971) unnamed region (raion). The basic results have already been presented in Lecture I, table III. Taking both his editions together, we can reconstruct the income distribution per head with reasonable exactitude. He remains a careless worker, but at least he has provided us with different misprints (which enables us to correct nearly all of them), and a very few new data. Here (see table I) is his basic table, which "is based on data of special sample investigations, which the Central Statistical Office undertakes systematically" (p. 109).

All these figures are repeated from the first edition, except that the "number of families" column is different. In the first edition this presented the strange result that the average percentages at the bottom did not agree with the detailed percentages in the table. This is now cleared up, and we only need to correct the misprints, as shown.

Korzhenevski generates from this his table 30, our table II

TABLE I (KORZHENEVSKI'S TABLE 29)
DISTRIBUTION OF FAMILIES BY TOTAL INCOME
AND SIZE OF FAMILY (IN % OF TOTAL NR. OF FAMILIES)

Total income	Nr. of families (thous.)	Nr. of families consisting of			
		2 people	3 people	4 people	5 or more
to 1200 R	15.5	58	42	–	–
1201–1800 R	92.9	45	35	20	–
1801–2400 R	120.0	36	29	23	(12)[a]
2401–3600 R	223.6	28	28	24	20
3601–4600 R	91.0	22	27	25	26
4601–6000 R	28.0	18	28	26	28
over 6000 R	4.0	10	32	28	30
Average	575.0	31.5	29.0[b] (29.5)	22.8	17.2[c] (16.0)

[a] The number 12 clearly belongs here. It occurs in the first edition, so its omission is a misprint.

[b] 29.5 is clearly correct. This mistake, which may or may not be a misprint, occurs in both editions.

[c] 17.2 is correct only if 12 is omitted.

here. Much of his interpolation is crude. Thus the 62.6 three-member families in R2401–3600 range from R801 to R1200 per capita. He has put exactly one quarter of them (15.6) in R801–900, where a slightly larger figure would have been better, since the mode of this row is clearly below R900. I have made such small corrections without discussion in table V.

But the 5+ group is a much more serious matter. In his table 30 Korzhenevski treats every single family in the 5+ group as averaging 6.0 members per family. He also lumps all these people into the per capita income groups suitable to exactly 6-member families, as if there were none of 5, 7 or 8. This treatment is very crude indeed, since he must have known

TABLE II (KORZHENEVSKI'S TABLE 30)
GROUPING OF FAMILIES OF WORKERS AND EMPLOYEES BY TOTAL INCOME AND FAMILY SIZE
(THOUS. FAMILIES)

Families by size of total income (R)	Total		Families by income per head (R)											
			up to 600		601–900		901–1200		1201–1500		1501–2100		over 2100	
	f	fm	f	fm	f	fm	f	fm	f	fm	f	fm	f	fm
up to 1200	15.5	37.5	15.5	37.5	–	–	–	–	–	–	–	–	–	–
1201–1800	92.9	255.5	51.1	171.9	41.8	83.6	–	–	–	–	–	–	–	–
1801–2400	120.0	385.6 [a]	42.0	194.8 [a]	34.8	104.4	43.2	86.4	–	–	–	–	–	–
2401–3600	223.6	794.8	44.8	268.6	69.2	260.0	47.0	141.0	31.3	62.6	31.3	62.6	–	–
3601–4800	91.0	346.6	–	–	23.6	141.6	22.8	91.2	24.6	73.8	12.0	24.0	8.0	16.0
4801–6000	28.0	109.6	–	–	5.8	34.8	2.0	12.0	7.3	29.2	7.8	23.4	5.1	10.2
over 6000	4.0	16.4	–	–	–	–	0.8	4.8	0.4	2.4	1.1	4.5	1.7	4.7
Total	575.0	1946.0 (1948.0)	153.4	672.8 (674.8)	175.2	624.4	115.8	335.4	63.6	168.0	52.2	114.5	14.8	30.9

[a] Clearly a mistake for 196.8 = 6 × 14.4 + 4 × 27.6; and so for 387.6.

f: families; fm: family members

TABLE III
LARGE FAMILIES IN KORZHENEVSKI

	Central Black Earth, urban, 1959	Korzhenevski	Ratio
singletons	122.4	130.0	1.06
2-member	155.5	182.5	1.18
3-member	160.2	170.1	1.06
4-member	129.4	131.1	1.01
5+member	111.5	91.8	0.824
5 member	69.1	(60.0)	(0.870)
6 member	27.8	(22.0)	(0.792)
7 member	10.5	(7.3)	(0.695)
8+member (set at 8.5, arbitrarily)	4.1	(2.5)	(0.610)

the exact figure, and the placement of, notably, 8+ families has a great effect on the result (below). To effect a correction, we inspect the 1959 census for a census region with approximately the right population and size distribution of families. Such a one is the Central Black Earth Region.[1] Its *urban* population was then 2181,000, while ours is 2076,000. Family sizes were as shown in table III (thousand).

The ratios in parentheses are extrapolated, with a view to generating such figures in the previous column as will add up to a sub-total of 91.8. The average size of 5+ families is 5.5, a substantially different figure from Korzhenevski's 6.0. He is so careless that I make bold to accept this correction. Doing so diminishes the amount of inequality, since it decreases the number of poor 8+ families.

[1] R.S.F.S.R. volume, pp. 440–1. It contains these oblasti: Bel'gorod, Voronezh, Kursk, Lipetsk, Tambov.

TABLE IV
CONTINUATION OF TABLE III

total family incomes	no. of 5+ families	(5)	(6)	(7)	(8+)
1801–2400	14.4	11.0	3.4	0.0	0.0
2401–3600	44.7	30.0	12.0	2.2	0.5
3601–4800	23.7	15.0	4.2	3.5	1.0
4801–6000	7.84	3.6	2.14	1.3	0.8
6001+	1.20	0.4	0.3	0.3	0.2
	91.84	60.00	22.04	7.30	2.50

We have now to fill in, arbitrarily but reasonably, a matrix of which we know the borders only (see table IV).

The singletons present also a problem. On p. 105 they are divided thus:

RO–720/10; R721–1200/50; R1201–1800/40;
R1801–2400/25; R2401+/5

And on p. 112 thus:

RO–600/4.6; R601–900/24.2; R901–1200/31.2;
R1201–1500/20.0; R1501–2100/32.5; R2101+/17.5.

Clearly Korzhenevski has crudely halved the previous R1201–1800 and R1801–2400 groups, and simply written 20, 20 + 12.5, 12.5 + 5. This is a most careless and implausible interpolation, which we must reject, simply substituting a better guess of our own. On the other hand, the redivision of the groups up to R1200 seem to rest on genuine extra information, and we accept this. In the first edition a similar error was made, on different figures.

We arrive at our final reconstruction, see table V.

In order to derive deciles we must unfortunately expand further and then manipulate – see table VI.

These results do not completely agree with our main results in Lecture I, table III. But if Korzhenevski's oblast' shows greater equality, this is only to be expected (cf. Lecture III). It is more worrying that his figures run 15% higher than the national average, and date from two years before.[2] I can only say that this variation is quite tolerable in view of the regional variations noted in Lecture III.

3. The third piece of evidence is from Raitsin 1970. On p. 186 he presents the figure that is here reproduced as fig. 2.

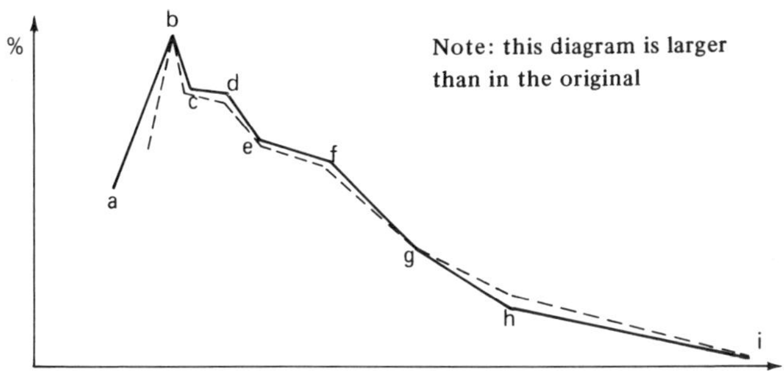

Fig. 2. (Raitsin's fig. 17). Factual (–) and computed (- -) by regression equation distribution of the members of the families of workers and employees by level of money income (my lettering).

Raitsin is interested not in the distribution itself, but in the relation of the main wage to the family income per head (this question is an obsession for Soviet statisticians). He arrives at

[2] Since the averages in table V went to the printer in June 1965, the newly published correct totals were also known at that time. Therefore the survey was taken in June 1964 at the latest.

TABLE V[a]

KORZHENEVSKI'S TABLE 30 REDONE

Nr. of members in family	Total nr. of families	<400	401–500	510–600	601–900
		nr. of families in each per capita income range			
			——4.6——	——————	5.4(720)18.8
1	130	0	1.0	3.6	24.2
			——9.0——	——————	
2	182.5	0	3.0	6.0	41.8
			——32.5——	——————	34.8(800)——
3	170.1	6.5	15.0	17.5	50.8
		18.6—(450)	——————	27.6	
4	131.1	12.0	15.6	18.6	53.7
		11.0	(480)———	30.0	(720)—15.0—
5	60.00	4.0	12.0	18.0	19.0
			——12.0——	———	4.2(800)2.14
6	22.04	3.4	5.0	7.0	5.1
			2.2—(514)—	—3.5—	(686)1.3(857)–
7	7.30	0.9	1.3	3.0	1.9
		0.8—(423)—	——0.6–	(565)—	(707)0.5
8+ = 8.5	2.50	0.7	0.6	0.5	0.7
no. of families	705.5				
no. of individuals		120.3	218.6	299.6	620.0

[a] In the bottom row of each pair are the final figures adopted. Above them are those original figures, derived from Tables I and IV, which require further interpolation. The horizontal lines indicate where

901–1200	1201–1500	1501–1800	1801–2400	2400+	Nr. of individuals
	——40.0——	————			
31.2	23.0	17.0	25.0	5.0	130.0
	{——62.6——	————	——5.04	+ 0.40	
43.2	{36.0	26.6	20.0	5.44	365.0
–62.6	24.6——	—(1600)—7.84—	(2000)——	1.28	
46.6	20.0	9.6	3.84	0.28	510.3
		——1.12	——		
22.8	7.28	1.00	0.12	0	524.4
(960) 3.6——	——0.4	——			
6.6	0.3	0.1	0	0	300.0
(1000)0.3					
1.54	0	0	0	0	132.2
—0.3					
0.2	0	0	0	0	51.1
0	0	0	0	0	21.3
392.2	185.6	——197.2	——	——	2034.0

the coverage of an original figure overlaps the chosen ruble intervals, and the numbers in parentheses show the boundaries of ruble intervals in these cases.

TABLE VI

THE DECILES IMPLIED BY KORZHENEVSKI

Income per head	< R400	401 – 500	501 – 600	601 – 700	701 – 800	801 – 900	901 – 1000	1001 – 1100	1101 – 1200	1201 – 1300	1301 – 1400	1401 – 1500	1500 +
Individuals	120.3	218.6	299.6	239	205	176	153	131.2	108	82	62.6	41	197.2
Cumulative		338.9	638.5	877.5	1082.5	1258.5	1411.5	1542.7	1650.7	1732.7	1795.3	1836.3	2033.5
Decile nrs.	1		2		3	4	5		6	7		8	9
Population per R1 [a]		1.70		2.60	2.50		2.25	1.95	1.68		1.41	1.20	0.20
Decile, R	444.8		526.1		588.6	671.5	766.3		877.2	1008.5		1180	1469.5

[a] These are my basic tools of interpolation, and must be set out in full. They are not, as so often in other work, simply the arithmetic means of the neighbouring rates, but make arbitrary allowances for likely curvature. They also take into account whether, for instance at the level of R500, we must add or subtract to find the nearest decile. Thus since the population at the second decile is 406.7 we must move upwards from 338.9 = R500. So the rate of population per R1 is closer to 2.996 than to 2.186. We add to R500 R (406.7–338.9) ÷ 2.60 = R26.1.

this formula, which he claims (pp. 186–7) to be stable over time and to have a very high confidence level:

$$\log D = -0.8925 + 1.3583 \log Z - 0.1961 \text{ Log } L,$$

where D is income per head of member, Z is wage of principal worker, and L is number of members in family.

Raitsin wishes planners and others, interested in future income distributions, to predict them via demographic projections (L) and the planned future wage (Z). He may well be right, but of course the outside observer has no figures for the relation of L to Z, so must rely upon R. and R.'s arithmetical multipliers (Lecture I table III). But we are in his debt for the by-products of his work: the statement that the last surveys by the C.S.O. were conducted in 1967 (p. 187), and fig. 2, which unlike that of R. and R. but like that of Loznevaya, is continuous back to zero along the horizontal axis.

Measuring in millimetres and rubles we find table VII.

It is clear from col. (iii) that R10 = 4 mm. This generates a superbly probable series of brackets from *c* to *i* (see our discussion of R. and R.'s figure above), but there is clearly something wrong with *a* and *b*. There is no series of brackets of which *b, c, d* and *e* could all be the midpoints, if it is accepted that there is *one* bracket of R10. For if *d* or *e* are midpoints of such a bracket, so must be *c* (and *e* or *d*). Rather than manipulate the brackets I prefer to think that point *b* is misplaced 2 mm. to the right; and have proceeded on this assumption. This may have something to do with the curious failure of the computed curve to give a value for *a*. Since some of the numbers in (vi) are doubtful, all of those in (vii) are doubtful, but *a, b* and *i* are more doubtful. Note, however, that if we accept that *b* and *c* are very narrow brackets *a* becomes a very broad one, and inequality goes up. It is possible that *b* is drawn out

TABLE VII
RAITSIN'S FIGURE ANALYSED

(i)	(ii)	(iii)	(iv)	(v)	(vi)	(vii)	(viii)	Columns	
Point	Height (mm)	Horiz. distance (mm)	Rubles at 4mm = R10	Suggested ruble bracket	(ii) × breadth of (v) (mm)	(vi) (%)	cumulative	(v) and (vii) expanded	
								R	%
a	20.0	9.0	?25	?20–30	? 80	7.4			
b	37.0	16.5	?35	?30–40	?148	13.7	21.1		
c	31.0	18.5	45	40–50	124	11.4	32.5		
d	30.5	22.5	55	50–60	122	11.3	43.8	70–80	9.0
e	25.5	26.5	65	60–70	102	9.4	53.2	80–90	8.5
f	23.0	34.5	85	70–100	276	25.4	78.6	90–100	7.9
g	13.5	45.0	110	100–120	108	10.0	88.6	100–110	6.0
h	6.5	56.5	140	120–160	104	9.6	98.2	110–120	4.0
i	?0.5	84.0	210	160–260	? 20	1.8			
					?1084	100.0			

TABLE VIII
THE DECILES IMPLIED BY RAITSIN

Decile nr.	1	2	3	4	5	6	7	8	9
% of population per ruble [a]	1.0	1.25	1.14	1.13	0.96	0.92	0.82	0.60	0.53
Rubles	32.6	39.1	47.8	56.7	66.7	77.6	89.1	102.3	122.6

[a] Cf. table VI.

of line to indicate the actual mode (R40) instead of the bracket midpoint. Col. (vi) indicates that had the diagram been accurate it would have subtended an area of 1000 mm^2. So a height of 2.5 mm. would represent 1% of the population at R10 = 4 mm. broad. Hence the unusually squat figure.

We arrive at the deciles of table VIII.

Raitsin's decile ratios are almost exactly those of our nation-wide estimate (Lecture I, table III), but are slightly less unequal. Like Korzhenevski's the absolute figures run 15–20% above ours but they may well date from the same or a later period. So we have again no reason to complain.

Raitsin's figure may be compared with a histogram of our nation-wide estimate (see fig. 3). Although the first and ninth deciles, being demarcation lines, are correctly placed, the rectangles that lie outside them have been guessed. The resemblance to Raitsin's figure is very striking.

4. Fourthly there is Raitsin's survey of an oblast', which he refers to and uses in three of his works listed. In 1966 he describes it as "a sample survey" (p. 848); in 1967 as "a sample survey in 1958 in one of the oblasti of the U.S.S.R." (p. 67). In 1970 he simply calls it "an example". Above all, he says it yields a quartile ratio of 1.80, decile 3.85, semi-decile

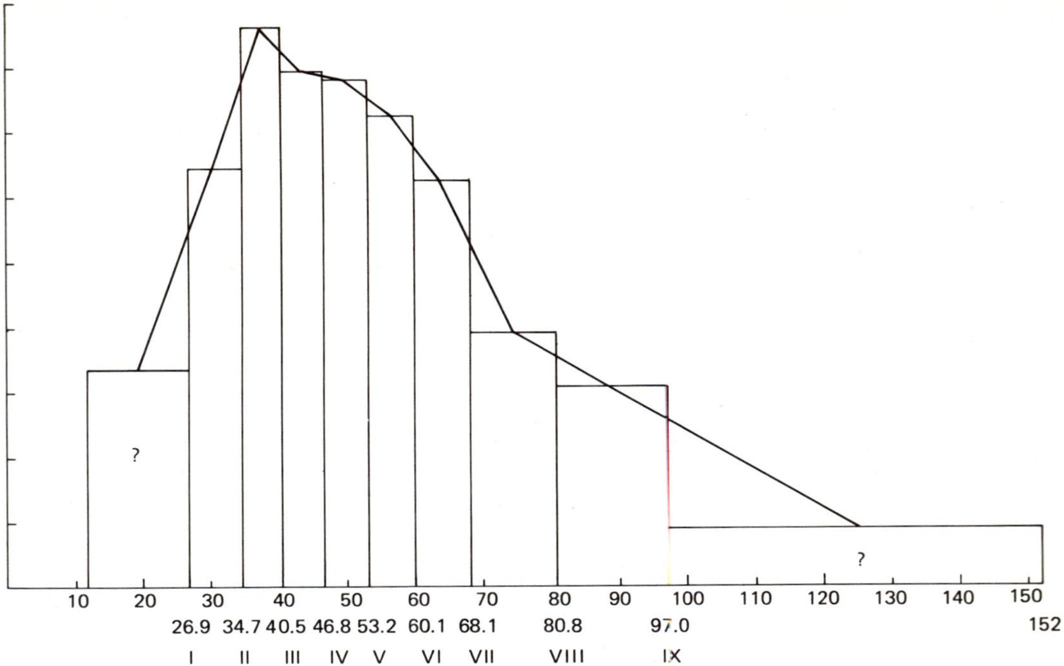

Fig. 3. The histogram implied by table I/III col. 4 (each square is 2% of the population).

TABLE IX
RAITSIN'S NUMERICAL EXAMPLE ANALYSED

Raitsin's percent-ages	Ruble intervals	Our interpolations $D_1 = 27.5$ $D_9 = 106$	27.3 105	27.0 104	Deciles, accepting $D_1 = 27.3$
15.5	14–21	5.5	5.5	5.5	$P_5 = 20.3$
	21–28	4.9	5.0	5.2	$D_1 = 27.3$
	28–35	5.1	5.0	4.8	
	35–40		9.5		$D_2 = 37.5$
28.2	40–45		9.7		$D_3 = 42.5$
	45–50		9.0		$D_4 = 48.0$
	50–55		8.7		$D_5 = 53.6$
	55–60		8.2		$D_6 = 59.8$
35.0	60–65		7.9		
	65–70		5.6		$D_7 = 66.3$
	70–75		4.6		
	75–80		2.85	2.80	$D_8 = 77.5$
	80–85		2.25	2.25	
10.0	85–90		1.90	1.85	
	90–95		1.60	1.60	
	95–100		1.40	1.50	
	100–05	1.20	1.30	1.40	
	105–10	1.15	1.25	1.35	$D_9 = 105.0$
	110–15	1.15	1.20	1.25	
	115–20	1.10	1.15	1.15	
8.7	120–25	1.10	1.10	1.05	
	125–30	1.05	1.00	0.95	$P_{95} = 126.0$
	130–35	1.00	0.90	0.85	
	135–40	0.95	0.80	0.70	
	140–50		1.10		
	150–60		0.60		
2.1	160–70		0.20		
	170–80		0.10		
	180–90		0.06		
	190–200		0.04		
0.5	200 +				

6.20 (pp. 851, 79). In table IX we present the original data and the range of plausible interpolation.

Limits are set as follows.

(i) The R100–105 bracket cannot have $< 1.2\%$, since 1.1% is the average per R5 over the whole range R100–140.

(ii) But if this figure is 1.4% $D_9 = 104$, so $D_1 = 27.0$. And if so the population of R28–35 can only be 4.8%, which is considerably less than that of the two lower seven-ruble brackets in the range R14–35. Therefore we are bounded by the values 1.2% and 1.4% in R100–105.

(iii) In any case the decline of frequency in the R100–140 range must be slow, since even 1.4 is close to the average of 1.1. So the brackets R130–135 and 135–140 must in any case contain comparatively many people, and P_{95} cannot lie outside R125–130. So $20.2 < P_5 < 21.0$.

(iv) Q_3 is given as $<$ R75. Q_1 is virtually given as $>$ R38. I have chosen R72 and R40.

This is the least credible of our reconstructions. The sharp rise between R28–35 and R35–40 is very uncomfortable, and so is the large population of R14–21. Yet it is not impossible that pensions and minimum wages prevent the "natural" decline of incomes below R14, and so put a step into the curve at its lower end.

APPENDIX II

OTHER DATA RELATING TO LECTURE IV

To begin with factor-shares, there were substantial shifts of a nature surely inexplicable by ordinary market reasoning during each world war in the U.K. Each time they were so big as to put beyond a doubt the further proposition that rich families suffered vis-à-vis poor families – such big reductions in rents and dividends, and increases in social security, could have had no other result. The Great Cost Inflation of 1969–date has had the same tendencies. We have, of course, better data on the latter years.

So the share of corporate profits in corporate value added fell precipitately during the first world war, and recovered partially after the great slump; and was stable at this, still distinctly lower, level until the great cost inflation of 1969–date when it fell again. Indeed, reckonings on the lines of table I, but using different definitions, show a fall in col. (vii) from 26.3% in 1961 to 21.2% in 1971. In these last years, however, corporate taxation has fallen and corporate subsidies, chiefly for regional purposes, have risen. As a result it is calculated that the rate of profit after these two taxes has remained the same.[1] But none of this affects the fall of distributed

[1] Wiles in *Economic Journal*, June 1973, p. 381; Mervyn King in *The Guardian*, 14 November 1973.

TABLE I

FACTOR-SHARES IN THE U.K., 1910–63[a]

(PERCENTAGES OF NATIONAL INCOME)

	(i) Farmers	(ii) Other self-employed	(iii) Corporate trading profits	(iv) Rent	(v) Wages[c]	(vi) Salaries[c]	(vii) $\frac{iii}{iii + v + vi}$ as percentage
1910–14	2.5	13.7	17.1	11.0	n.a.	n.a.	23.5
1921–24	2.1	15.1	13.0	6.8	44.0[b]	19.0[b]	17.1
1925–29	1.3	14.8	12.5	7.5	42.2	21.7	16.4
1930–34	1.6	13.4	12.5	9.0	41.1	22.4	16.5
1935–38	1.6	11.6	15.0	8.8	40.6	22.4	19.2
1946–49	2.9	9.4	16.8	4.0	42.3	24.6	20.1
1950–54	2.8	7.8	18.0	3.9	42.4	24.1	21.3
1955–59	2.3	6.9	18.0	4.5	42.2	26.1	21.4
1960–63	2.1	6.3	17.9	5.1	40.4	28.2	20.7

[a] From S.H. Feinstein, "Evolution . . .", in I.E.A. Conference on Income Distribution, 1968, pp. 116-7, unless otherwise stated; includes Eire in 1910–14.

[b] Interpolated from E.H. Phelps Brown, Pay and Profits, Manchester 1968, p.3.

[c] Interpolated from Emile Primorac, Ph.D. thesis at London University 1966, p. 90, unless otherwise stated.

TABLE II

FACTOR-SHARES IN THE U.K., 1938–72 (INDEX NUMBERS, EARLIER YEAR = 100)

	1938–49 [c]		1949–68 [a]		1968–72 [d]	
Distributed property income	132		355		124	
Undistributed corporate profits	355		324		154	
All property income		183		388		–
Earnings of: sole traders	166		206		156	
professionals	205		225		147	
farmers	455		186		148	
All mixed income		201		207		154
Salaries	203		(270)[b]		(149)	
Wages	247		(308)[b]		(157)	
Forces' pay	314		243		159	
All earned income		232		349		146
Social security benefits	257		–			
War pensions etc.	321		–			
All social income		267		540	159	

[a] National Income Blue Book, 1969, pp. 4, 5, 24; Annual Abstract 1960, pp. 233–4.

[b] The actual value indices are 443 and 291; but I give per capita figures in view of the great proportionate shift in numbers. The 308 is the index of all manual workers' earnings, published everywhere. For salaries I take the implied index in manufacturing industry, 1949–55 (1957 Blue Book, p. 10), and the explicit index, 1955–date, for all salaries in the D.E.P.'s Statistics on Income, Prices, Employment and Production, monthly.

[c] Dudley Seers, The Levelling of Incomes since 1938, Oxford 1956.

[d] 1973 Blue Book; D.E.P. Gazette Sep. 1973; British Labour Statistics 1971. The figures in parentheses are per capita; note that the number of employed persons has fallen.

profits in table II. And this cannot be explained by a reduction in capital-intensity, nor, surely, by those curious macro-economic, ex post, two-sector elasticities of substitution that high growth theory has made fashionable. Each of these adjectives is meant as a reproach: a true elasticity with explanatory force would be ex ante, micro- and with respect to many inputs. It would be a parameter in the mind of a particular entrepreneur contemplating factor prices and technology in his own business. We have hardly any such data. Within the reward to labour, furthermore, wages have gained steadily on salaries if we take them per head, after income tax.

But factor-shares are not our main concern. Here is an international comparison of business wages and salaries, made by the Centre d'Etudes des Revenus et des Couts in late 1968.[2] The C.E.R.C. allocated points to various jobs as follows (p. 23):

65– 75 points	Cleaner
80– 90	Messenger
90– 120	Worker P1
100– 115	Typist
100– 150	Worker P2
120– 150	Shorthand/typist
120– 150	Clerk, accounts
140– 220	Accountant
150– 250	Secretary
150– 250	Worker P3
250– 400	Foreman
300– 500	Shop manager
350– 550	Technical or commercial employee
550– 700	Production manager

[2] *La hiérarchie des salaries*, Paris, Documentation Francaise, 1972.

400– 900	Engineer, R and D
500–1000	Chief buyer
700–1500	Factory director
700–2000	Sales director
700–2000	Technical director
900–2200	Commercial director

I summarize the main results in table III.

The columns 1500/100 and 1500/80 are the ones that count for our purposes. They are not, as the authors point out, the same kind of thing as a semi-decile ratio, since the "1500" grades and the "100" grades may bear different proportions to the total labour force in each country. But the C.E.R.C. feels that their "1500" jobs are on the average at about the first semi-decile (p. 39); which is a long way short of the top.

So much for job comparisons. We have also figures for the top centile, whatever the job. Table IV is from Lydall 1968. It tries to confine itself to males only, because in practice 10 years ago only males got top salaries. It distorts our data to include the top centile of women; the degree of distortion, however, is only known for the U.S.A.

The movement over time is given by Routh 1965, pp. 53, 54, 62. The top centile of men's and women's earned income after tax as a multiple of the median fell as follows: 1911/12, 4.64; 1958/9, 3.24. The 1911/12 figure would appear, like the others, to exclude all parts of Ireland – an important point – but it is certainly a "heroic" estimate. *Within* the professions we find a similar equalization. The growth of the highest decile from 1913/14 to 1955/6 compares with the growth of the median as follows (%):

barristers	275 and 596	solicitors	282 and 434
doctors	295 and 622	dentists	328 and 674

TABLE III

JOB COMPARISONS IN SIX ADVANCED CAPITALIST COUNTRIES, 1968

(STRAIGHT MULTIPLES)

	Net remuneration [a]				Labour cost to enterprise [b]				Net remuneration after income tax [c]			
	1500/100	1500/80	800/100	500/100	1500/100	1500/80	800/100	500/100	1500/100	1500/80	800/100	500/100
U.K.	12.0	13.9	6.1	3.7	9.3	10.6	5.0	3.1	–	9.4	4.7	2.97
Italy	11.9	12.9	6.0	3.7	9.4	10.2	5.0	3.4	–	9.7	5.0	3.29
France	10.7	11.7	5.9	3.9	8.9	9.7	5.1	3.6	–	8.6	5.0	3.54
German F.R.	10.4	11.2	5.2	3.0	8.5	9.2	4.4	2.8	–	8.3	4.4	2.75
Netherlands	10.4	11.4	5.5	3.4	7.7	8.4	4.3	2.9	–	7.0	4.1	2.88
U.S.A.	7.8	8.6	4.2	2.8	7.0	7.7	3.8	2.7	–	6.9	3.8	2.65

[a] Fringe benefits in kind + bonuses + wage or salary.

[b] (a) + employer's social contributions + employee's social contributions.

[c] (a) – income tax on childless married couple.

Source: Hierarchie . . . . , pp. 8, 20, 26 .

TABLE IV
PROPORTION OF TOP CENTILE TO MEDIAN
(WAGES AND SALARIES, GROSS OF TAX, ALL AGES, OCCUPATIONS AND INDUSTRIES, MALES ONLY, UNLESS OTHERWISE STATED)

Lydall's table no.	Date	Country	Specification	Proportion
AU-1	1957	Austria		3.64
CZ-1	1964	Czechoslovakia	incl. females [c], socialist sector only	2.18
FN-1	1960	Finland		5.15
FR-4	1961	France	non-farm [a]	6.10
GE-2	1957	German F.R.		3.42
ME-1	1960	Mexico	incl. females [c]	16.70
PO-1	1960	Poland	incl. females [c], socialist sector only	3.08
SW-11	1964	Sweden	incl. females [c]	3.67
SW-13	1964	Sweden	incl. females [c]	3.90
UK-5	1958–9	U.K.	incl. females [c]	3.72
UK-5	1958–9	U.K.	incl. females [c]	3.80
US-1	1959	U.S.A.		3.80 (est.)
US-3	1959	U.S.A.	incl. females [c]	3.94
US 9	1959	U.S.A.	incl. females [c], non-farm [a]	3.90

[a] And therefore understates the inequality.
[b] I.e. incl. state farmers, excl. peasants.
[c] And therefore overstates the inequality.

In absolute terms the medians in these professions cluster about the top centile of all earned incomes in 1911/12 and 1958/9.

Routh also provides information about the top millile. In 1911/12 it was 13.93 times the median and in 1958/9, 5.60 times, after tax. In the latter year its real purchasing power, as reckoned by Bowley's and the London and Cambridge cost of living indices, had fallen by 22%. While Routh's other results may well be explained by the expansion of higher education and other orthodox market forces, I find this striking information about the millile a confirmation of Lecture IV: it can surely only be explained by appeals to sentimental motivation, administrative action by bodies nominally competing on a market, and the theory that senior and junior people are non-competing groups.

More modern figures are very scarce. An official series dates only from 1968. So leaving a ten-year gap for the more laborious to fill, I present the results of the Department of Employment's New Earnings Survey since its inception, where there is continuity:

TABLE V
U.K., GROSS EARNINGS OF FULL-TIME ADULT MEN, £ PER WEEK

	Sept. 1968		April 1972	
	Median	Upper quartile	Median	Upper quartile
General manager, divisional manager	52.8	77.8	68.5	88.5
Company secretary	39.5	57.9	55.7	70.9
Works manager, production manager	34.5	43.2	47.7	61.0
Marketing, advertising, sales manager	43.2	57.6	57.5	72.2
Engineer - civil, structural or municipal	37.0	47.1	50.6	62.3
Engineer - electrical, electronic	32.0	40.9	47.1	57.4

Table V (continued)

	Sept. 1968 Median	Sept. 1968 Upper quartile	April 1972 Median	April 1972 Upper quartile
Engineer - mechanical	33.4	40.9	47.8	59.6
University academic staff	41.0	49.9	65.0	79.7
Accountant	31.9	41.9	44.7	60.1
Surveyor	33.6	42.3	42.6	55.1
	Index numbers			
Unweighted average of above	100		139.0	
		100		133.5
Male manual (mean)	100		145.1	
Female manual (mean)	100		150.9	

Source: *New Earnings Survey*, 1968, p. 19; 1972, p. 139.

Simultaneously capital holdings have been much equalized (Lecture II/6). But this owes much to the chances (?) of a dividend freeze and a boom in land and house prices.

APPENDIX III

MY PRINCIPLES OF INTERPOLATION

(i) All formulae for correcting as opposed to describing distributions (lognormal, Pareto, etc.) are empirical approximations. To describe them as more, or to give them a priori validity, is sheer mysticism. Each distribution is what it is.

(ii) Therefore whatever data there are, e.g. the midpoints, widths and heights of histogram panels, must be accepted absolutely. But unfortunately we must interpolate between these data to obtain comparability. This inescapably involves elements of (i), and I have chosen these assumptions or principles:

(iii) If we do not interpolate we get no results. So we must seldom hesitate to do so.

(iv) It is wrong to prefer a priori the simplest possible interpolation. Such a preference leads, say in the division of a histogram panel wholly on one side of the mode, to the assumption that each subdivision has the average value of the whole. See fig. 1. This is a good instance of maximum simplicity being outright wrong.

(v) All distributions are unimodal (this is certainly false for some small samples).

(vi) There shall be as few points of inflexion as is compatible with (ii) and (iv) (this has many empirical exceptions, even in

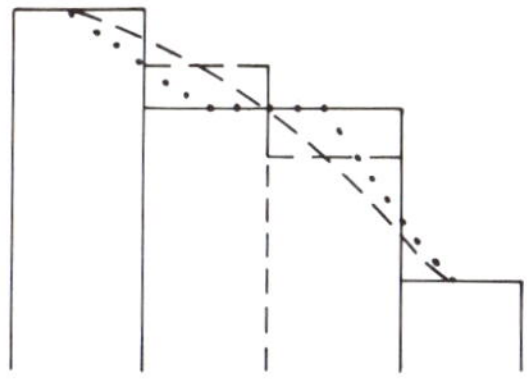

Fig. 1.

rather large samples, and the lognormal distribution itself has two points of inflexion).

(vii) Subject to (ii), (v) and (vi) interpolation shall be Paretian downward from both sides of the mode. E.g. the slope across a given histogram panel, that needs to be divided, shall be so arranged as to produce as straight a line as possible between the new points and their neighbours in other panels, with the axes set out logarithmically:

—— before interpolation
· · · · wrong interpolation as in (iv)
– – – a better interpolation as in (vii)

There is no very good evidence for this assumption either; but almost anything is an improvement on (iv). See (ix).

(viii) When two or more consecutive panels must be divided, note how the "nicest" interpolation in one panel leads to a "nasty" one in the next (see fig. 2). The line – – – keeps a "nice" relation between d_1 and c_2, but brings down c_1. This is tolerable so long as b_2 is kept low, but that pushes up b_1 to unreasonable heights, and makes an unusually flat mode. If b_1 were reduced to the line ...., this would have repercussions right down to c_2, which would cease to be "nicely" related to d_1, and produce virtual equality between d_1 and d_2. Alterna-

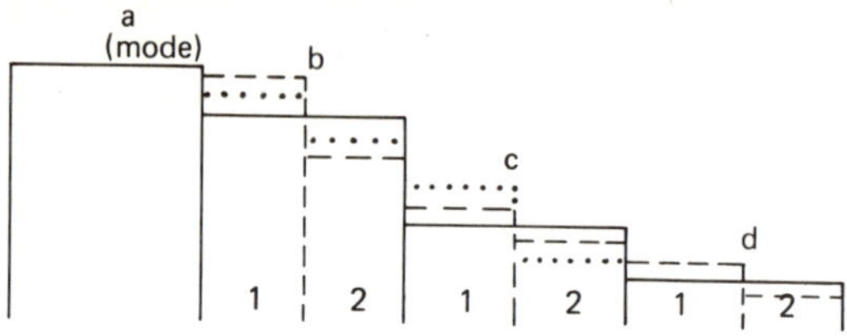

Fig. 2.

tively we could keep b_1 and b_2 ....., and c_1 and c_2 – – – but accept two points of inflexion: b_2/c_1 and d_1/d_2. But this violates rule (vi). This effect sets surprisingly narrow limits to the interpolative imagination.

(ix) If interpolation is Paretian subject to (viii), we get little iso-elastic stretches, each of different elasticity. We get by no means a wholly iso-elastic curve all the way down from the mode, nor do we aim at any such thing (see Lecture I, section 2).

(x) Since nearly all distribution graphs are the midpoints of histogram panels connected up, it is far better to identify and draw these histograms, and calculate their areas, than to use a planimeter. In particular the planimeter cuts out half the bottom and half the top panel, which lie outside the area vertically covered by the graph. If these panels are broad, much population is missed at the all-important extremes.

(xi) When interpolating near the boundary of two panels we must accept neither the frequency within (the whole of) either panel, nor the arithmetic mean of both such frequencies, but allow for likely curvature. See Appendix I, table VI.

BIBLIOGRAPHY

Atkinson, A.B., *Journal of Economic Theory*, Sept. 1970. *Unequal Shares*, London 1972.

Bell, Daniel, *The Public Interest,* Fall 1972.

Bergson, Abram, *The Real National Income of Soviet Russia since 1928,* Cambridge, Mass., Harvard, 1961. *The Structure of Soviet Wages,* Cambridge, Mass., Harvard, 1946.

Bronfenbrenner, Martin, *Economic Development and Cultural Change,* April 1955. and Daniel H. Garnick, *Economic Development and Cultural Change,* July 1963.

Bukharin, Nikolai, *Oekonomik der Transformationsperiode,* Hamburg 1922.

Cline, Wlliam R., *Potential Effects of Income Redistribution on Economic Growth,* New York 1972.

Currie, Lauchlin, *Accelerating Development,* New York 1966.

Dean, Edwin, *The Supply Response of African Farmers*, Amsterdam 1966.

"F.E.S.": *Family Expenditure Survey,* Department of Employment, London, annual.

Friedman, Milton, *A Theory of the Consumption Function,* Princeton, N.J., 1957.

ul-Haq, Mahbub, "The Crisis in Development Strategies". Lecture to the International Development Conference, Washington D.C., 20 April 1972.

Illich, Ivan, *Deschooling Society*, New York 1971.

Kapustin, I. and N.P. Kuznetsova, *Ekonomicheskie Nauki,* 1/1972.

Keynes, John Maynard, *The General Theory of Employment, Interest and Money*, London 1936.

Kirsch, Leonard J., *Soviet Wages,* Cambridge, Mass., 1972.

Korzhenevski, I.I., *Osnovnye Zakonomernosti Razvitiya Sprosa v SSSR,* Moscow 1971; and the first edition, 1965.

Little, Ian M.D., *Welfare Economics,* Oxford 1950.

Loznevaya, M., *Sotsialisticheski Trud,* 10/1968.

Lydall, Harold, *The Structure of Earnings,* Oxford 1968.

McNamara, Robert S., *One Hundred Countries, Two Billion People,* New York 1973.

Mozhina, M., *Trud i Zarabotnaya Plata,* 10/1961.

"Nar. Khoz.": *Narodnoye Khozyaistvo,* the Soviet statistical yearbook. The year is the year in the title, not that of publication.

Nicholson, R.J., *Lloyds Bank Review,* 1967.

Pryor, Frederick, *Slavic Review,* Sept. 1972.

Rabkina, N.E. and I.M. Rimashevskaya, *Osnovy Differentsiatsii Zarabotnoi Platy i Dokhodov Naselenia,* Moscow 1972.

Raitsin, V.Ya. (with E.M. Poberezhskaya), *Ekonomika i Matematicheskie Metody,* 6/1966. *Normativnye Metody Planirovaniya Urovnya Zhizni,* Moscow 1967. *Matematicheskie Metody i Modeli Planirovaniya Urovnya Zhizni,* Moscow 1970.

Rawls, John, *A Theory of Justice,* Oxford 1972.

Routh, Guy, *Occupation and Pay in Great Britain,* Cambridge 1965.

Sarkisyan, G.S., *Uroven', Tempi i Proportsii Realnykh Dokhodov pri Sotsializme,* Moscow 1972, and N.P. Kuznetsova, *Potrebnosti i Dokhod Sem'i,* Moscow 1967.

Sen, Amartya K., *On Economic Inequality*, Oxford 1973.

Stark, T., *The Distribution of Personal Income in the U.K.,* London 1972.

Wagener, Hans-Jürgen, *Wirtschaftswachstum in Unterentwickelten Gebieten,* Berlin 1972. *Revue de l'Est,* April 1973.

Wilber, Charles K., *The Soviet Model and Underdeveloped Countries,* Chapel Hill 1969.

Wiles, Peter, *Communist International Economics,* Oxford 1969. and Stefan Markowski, *Soviet Studies*, Jan. and April 1971, in *Distribuzione del reddito nella pianificazione economica,* ISDEE, Trieste, 1974.

Wootton, Barbara, *The Social Foundations of Wage Policy*, London 1955.

Zacchia, Carlo, in *Distribuzione del reddito nella pianificazione economica*, ISDEE, Trieste, 1974.